The Old Man and the Knee

The Old Man and the Knee

How to be a Golden Oldie

CHRISTOPHER MATTHEW

Little, Brown

LITTLE, BROWN

First published in Great Britain in 2017 by Little, Brown

1 3 5 7 9 10 8 6 4 2

Copyright © Christopher Matthew 2017

The moral right of the author has been asserted.

A CIP catalogue record for this book
is available from the British Library.

'The South Country' from *Sonnets and Verse* by
Hilaire Belloc reprinted by permission of Peters Fraser & Dunlop
(www.petersfraserdunlop.com) on behalf of the Estate of Hilaire Belloc

ISBN 978-1-4087-1043-2

Typeset in Minion by M Rules
Printed and bound in Great Britain by
Clays Ltd, St Ives plc

Papers used by Little, Brown are from well-managed forests
and other responsible sources.

MIX
Paper from
responsible sources
FSC
www.fsc.org   FSC® C104740

Little, Brown
An imprint of
Little, Brown Book Group
Carmelite House
50 Victoria Embankment
London EC4Y 0DZ

An Hachette UK Company
www.hachette.co.uk

www.littlebrown.co.uk

In memory of my friends
who didn't make the cut

Contents

The Big Question

'What's it like being old, Grandpa?'

'Ludo, how many more times must I tell you? I'm not old. Not yet, anyway.'

'You're *quite* old.'

'Compared with you, perhaps.'

'Compared with lots of people. Including Granny.'

'Granny was born with the gift of everlasting youth and beauty.'

'She's very lucky.'

'She is. And she looks after herself. She dresses well and doesn't try and make herself seem younger than she is. She has lots of friends, she is very popular and she's always busy. And she laughs a lot. She's full of beans.'

'You look quite young, too, Grandpa. For your age.'

'I don't always feel that young. Especially first thing in the morning. I am sometimes so stiff in the limbs that I can hardly move.'

'Is that because of your age?'

'I presume so. My back is stiff because the cartilage between the discs is crumbling, which means the bones are slightly out of alignment and rub together, which is the cause of lumbago.'

'What's lumbago?'

'Pain in the muscles and joints of the lower back.'

'And in your leg.'

'And in my leg.'

'But you can still play golf.'

'But not tennis. Or some of the things I used to do when I was younger. Like squash. And skiing.'

'You still swim in the sea in the summer.'

'As long as there aren't too many people around. I'm not a pretty sight nowadays without clothes. There's a lot of loose skin flapping around, and my legs wouldn't win any beauty contests.'

'And you still work.'

'If you can call sitting at a desk tapping away at the keyboard of a laptop working.'

'Someone said his grandfather hadn't got a very good memory. Have you got a good memory?'

'I forget people's names. Sometimes the names of people I know quite well. I spend a lot of time going through the alphabet in the hope that one of the letters will give me a clue.'

'Does that work?'

'Not often. The name usually comes back to me when I least expect it. Usually when I'm thinking of something completely different. I also do that thing that a lot of old people do, which is walking into a room and wondering why I'm there. And I often can't remember where I have put things, like my reading glasses.'

'That happens to me, too.'

'Since when did you start wearing reading glasses?'

'I meant my iPad.'

'Perhaps it's not such an old person thing after all.'

'Perhaps you're not an old person.'

'I hope not. Not yet, anyway.'

'So that's all right, then.'

'For the time being, anyway. Cross fingers.'

'Cross fingers.'

Snap in the Celery

Before we go any further, I'd like to get one thing straight. I am not old. I know what old is, and I'm not it.

My grandmother was old, and lived to a great age. I couldn't say exactly how great, for the simple reason that I never dared to ask her how old she was. It wasn't the sort of thing children asked grown-ups. Others did, apparently, and her answer was always the same: 'As old as my tongue and a little older than my teeth.'

As it happens, I had an intensive hour with a dental hygienist only the other day. She gave my last remaining lot a serious seeing to with dental scaler, jet spray and polisher, and followed it up with a lesson on brushing, flossing and TePe interdental work.

I don't think that in all the decades of having teeth – grown-up ones, anyway – I have ever been taught the best way to ensure they are in tip-top condition. I had always imagined that a brisk scrub round with a brush twice a day would suffice.

Given that I have more amalgam in my mouth than actual

teeth, I assumed it was only a matter of time before the whole lot started to fall apart, if not out.

A friend of mine in his eighties was told by his dentist, 'Well, there's not a lot more I can do for your teeth; all you've got to worry about now are your gums.'

Post-war dentistry was decidedly vague on dental hygiene. I don't ever remember being told that sweets rotted your teeth (not that we had that many sweets in those days, what with them being on ration and so on), so it came as quite a surprise when, as a boy, I was told I had a cavity in one of my molars and that it would need filling.

Nor at that stage did I have any idea how painful it would be. Dental anaesthesia was as far in the future as space travel – and about as unimaginable. So, too, were high-speed electric drills. Is it my imagination, or did the dentist operate a museum-quality version with a foot pedal? It certainly felt like it. Like the mills of God, the large drill heads ground slowly, but, unlike them, they ground extremely large, and extremely painful.

Extraction took place under gas. A black rubber mask was placed over one's face and mouth, a tap was turned on, there was a faint hissing sound and the next thing one knew one's tongue was exploring an enormous crater.

Nitrous oxide – also known as laughing gas – is now commonly used by certain types of young people as a way of achieving short-lived euphoria. (English parks are knee-deep in empty silver bulbs.) As a boy in the dentist's chair, I don't remember feeling anything very much – though a school friend of mine told me that he once had a very rude dream while under the influence of laughing gas and woke up to find the doctor and his nurse sniggering together.

Another characteristic of post-war dentistry was the conviction (in the practice I visited, anyway) that even if it was perfectly obvious that you had too many teeth to fit into your mouth, that was no reason not to try, with the help of various expandable plates, to make them do so. Which explains why so many of my contemporaries ended up snaggle-toothed. They say you can tell the age of a horse by looking at its teeth. My friends, too.

These days it is rare to see anyone under the age of sixty with anything other than a gleaming set of perfect ivories. There is no way I can turn the dental clock back, but, as my hygienist reminded me, I am very lucky to have as many teeth as I do, and now that I know how to clean them properly I hope to keep as many as I possibly can.

My fifteen-year-old granddaughter Tug (her real name's Tamara, but everyone calls her Tug because she is tall and beautiful and always seems to be tugging a string of girls behind her) spent more than two years with a ferocious-looking wire device in her mouth and now has a smile as white, bright and perfect as any of those models back in the fifties whose pictures one used to see in magazines, advertising SR toothpaste. In fact, it was this amazing transformation in her looks that urged me into this brisk walk down my own dental lane.

She said, 'Listening to you is like reading a history book.'

'I suppose it is,' I said. 'But then, when you think about it, your life is as far removed from mine as mine was from my parents. Both of them were born shortly after the death of Queen Victoria. When they were children, Louis Blériot made the first flight across the Channel; the streets were still crowded with horse-drawn vehicles (though a handful of brave people were driving cars built by Herbert Austin of the Wolseley Sheep Shearing Machine Company); and street lights were lit by a man holding a lighted wick on a long pole.'

'Cool,' she said. 'Your parents were historical.'

'Cooler still,' I said, 'is when you think that my grandmother was born just after the Crimean War, and her mother was born the same year Darwin's *Beagle* was launched at Woolwich Dockyard.'

'That's *really* historical,' she said.

'Almost as historical as my great-grandmother. She was a Polish concert pianist, so she might have known Chopin.'

My granddaughter is not often reduced to silence by anything, or anyone, but this passing suggestion that I might have seriously artistic blood in my veins was a rare exception.

A day or two later she rang to say that she had been told to write something about a historical figure, and why didn't she write about me?

'Cool,' I said.

I certainly didn't mean it. Never once have I thought of myself as being from a bygone age. I'm only seventy-eight, for goodness' sake. Mind you, it is not uncommon for people of my age to bump themselves up a year or two. I myself have been heard to say I'm nearly eighty. I can't think why. Unless it's in the hope of getting a reply along the lines of, 'Well, you certainly don't look it.' Fat chance of that. Soon after I hit seventy, I was chatting with an old boy in our village, and for some reason he asked me how old I was. When I told him, he said, 'Christ, I thought you were older than that.'

I suppose that to a fifteen-year-old I *could* seem to be a

creature from a bygone age. But that does not mean I'm old. Getting on a bit, perhaps. Not quite as young as I once was. No spring chicken. But definitely not old. Or even elderly. Not yet over the hill, but happily on the brow. Hardly historical. Yet.

I have to admit that I can't remember what it's like to pay for an NHS prescription or for a ticket on a London bus or on the Underground – not counting the day last week when I stupidly left my Freedom Pass behind, and discovered it costs the thick end of a fiver to travel eleven stops on the Circle Line.

I am missing a few vital organs (or they certainly would be vital if I were fifty years younger), and my left leg still gives me gyp following two hip replacements. I quite often mislay my glasses, I sometimes have a quick snooze at around four in the afternoon, and whatever my wife may say, I do not suffer from Age-Activated Attention Deficit Disorder. If I choose to do two or three little jobs in addition to, and at the same time as, the one I was originally planning to do, that is because I want to, not because I am losing the plot.

I have a tendency to utter a slight 'oof' noise when I sit down in an armchair, and a breathy groan when I stand up. This does not necessarily signify that I am in any pain – it's merely something a lot of people do after a certain age. Like breaking wind when they bend over to tie a shoelace.

To sum up, I am enjoying late middle age, more or less as I have been doing for the last quarter of a century. I go for brisk walks every day with the dog; I play quite a lot of golf; I sail in my *Swallows and Amazons*-style dinghy; my bowels have never been in better shape; I am still turning out books; and here's the clincher: with some exceptions, people don't think I'm old.

I know this for a fact, because on crowded Tube trains no one ever offers me a seat. This is mainly, of course, because they are all far too preoccupied with their iPhones, and, even if they were to drag their eyes away for a nanosecond, the thought that someone might be more in need of a seat than them would never enter their minds. Am I upset? Am I irritated by their carelessness and bad manners? Do I want to sit down anyway? Far from it. I am happy to stand the whole way, even if I do have do so with a rucksack jammed into the small of my back and a semi-bearded face with bad breath inches from my own.

Not only am I invariably the first out through the open doors, but I take the entire length of the nearest up escalator at a trot that I can only describe as brisk.

Q.E.D., I think.

Hello: one of my front teeth has started to come loose . . .

Mustn't Grumble

The English are well known as the masters, and mistresses, of understatement – often in the direst of circumstances. When in 1912, as the situation in Scott's expedition became ever more grim, Captain Oates left the tent on the Ross Ice Shelf and, in the hope of saving the lives of his companions by sacrificing his own, walked into a blizzard with the words 'I am just going outside and may be some time', he set the standard for understatement for generations to come.

One can't help but feel that, if it hadn't been for Oates's pronouncement at that moment of high tragedy, one wouldn't hear English men and women replying, when asked how they are after a certain age or following some personal disaster or tragedy, 'Mustn't grumble,' or, another favourite, 'Worse things happen at sea.'

My grandmother always used to say, 'Sitting up and taking nourishment.'

It didn't invite further enquiry, though it did rather suggest that one might have taken to one's bed – or anyway one's armchair. Possibly indefinitely.

But, then, the older generation has long been equipped with a vocabulary of euphemistic ways of saying 'We know we are getting older, but we're making the best of it and we don't want to go into details.' It's as if they, and we, had returned to the code of good manners as practised in Victorian times, when no one quite meant what they said and everyone knew *exactly* what they meant.

'Feeling one's age' was another popular response among the elderly back in the sixties.

'How are you?' a friend would ask of my mother if she bumped into her in Boots Library.

'Oh, you know. Feeling my age,' she'd say. (She was probably only in her sixties at the time.) And though she might have been suffering at the time from agonising sciatica, or wondering whether to have all her remaining teeth removed to save on future dentistry, as many did in those days, they'd both laugh knowingly.

Do I feel mine? I wonder. Difficult to say. I don't really know how I'm supposed to be feeling at the age I am. Whether my mother felt any different at seventy-eight than I do is hard to judge since it's not a subject she ever thought to raise. I am only sorry she is no longer here for us to compare notes.

Dismissive phrases of this kind are still commonly heard from both sexes – the main difference being that when women say 'Mustn't grumble' they mean it, and when men say it, they promptly go ahead and do so.

Women are long suffering; men are only too happy to let you have the full details with both barrels, and, the older we all get, the more obvious it is that when it comes to putting up with the travails of old age, women have the Oates spirit with knobs on.

Grumpy Old Men was a hugely popular series back in the noughties. None of the participants was what you'd call old at the time, but there's nothing blokes of a certain age like more than sitting around listening to other blokes beefing about life's little irritations – compulsory tipping, answering mobiles at the table, that kind of thing.

Grumpy Old Women didn't work half as well, for the simple reason that women are nothing like as good at grumbling as men.

Disraeli's maxim 'Never complain, never explain' has over the years been adopted by any number of important characters, from prime ministers to pop stars, but it could as easily be the motto for women of a certain age.

P. G. Wodehouse – himself the master of understatement – put it more elegantly.

'At the age of eleven or thereabouts,' he wrote in *Uneasy Money*, 'women acquire a poise and an ability to handle difficult situations which a man, if he is lucky, manages to achieve somewhere in the later seventies.'

Their good fortune can be ascribed as much to their nature as to the nurture of the schools they attend – in particular girls' boarding schools. Women are blessed with a God-given talent for friendship (with men to some extent, though chaps are often incapable of enjoying close friendships with women unless sex is involved) and the close relationships they establish at school with their contemporaries, which sometimes begin the moment they arrive, can last a lifetime, and very often do.

From the day Mrs Matthew and her chums left school nearly sixty years ago, a gang of them have kept in close touch through marriages, divorces, death and dramas.

Girls who went to boarding schools in her era are particularly good at this. The eccentric – not to say harsh – conditions in which they spent most of their teenage years bound them together for life, and they look back on those days of freezing dormitories, terrible food and equally terrible members of staff with humour and a weird affection that has been perfectly captured in *Terms & Conditions*, Ysenda Maxtone Graham's glorious history of life in girls' boarding schools from 1939 to 1979.

Speaking about it with one of the old girls she interviewed for the book, I wondered why no one had thought of doing an old boys' version.

'It wouldn't work,' she said. 'Boys turn into men and other things come along to occupy their minds. A lot of them hated their schools and don't wish to be reminded of them; and anyway, once they've left school, men go their separate ways and on the whole don't keep up with their old friends.'

I was reminded of a story told to me by an old school friend, a successful solicitor, about how he went to a school reunion and bumped into a man who had been a contemporary of his, and something of a friend.

'Hello,' said the solicitor. 'How nice to see after all these years. What are you up to these days?'

The man replied, 'I'm the chairman of a big multi-national. What have you done with your life?'

An old girl of another school overheard our conversation.

'Speaking for myself,' she said, 'the older I get, the more I need my old friends.'

To my regret, I have lost touch with all too many of my best friends at school, and, for all my good intentions, I have never done a thing about making plans to see them again. I never go to school reunions and, were I to do so, it's all Lombard Street to a China orange that none of them would be there.

I suggested to Mrs Matthew that perhaps in old age men don't need their old friends as much as women do.

'Men are hopeless at keeping in touch,' she said. Brisk and to the point as usual.

State of Play

Are we making the best of the time that's been left to us? It was a question my old friend Alan Coren and I would often ask ourselves. We spoke about many things, and we laughed a lot together, and talked about our childhood, and what we would do when we were old, and Alan would quote the last lines of Belloc's poem 'The South Country':

> I will hold my house in the high wood
> Within a walk of the sea,
> And the men that were boys when I was a boy
> Shall sit and drink with me.

But thoughts of death were often on our minds. He would say that he didn't mind the thought of dying, but he did worry about leaving Annie, his wife, behind and how she would cope.

Something of a hypochondriac, he would always be finding some new pain or condition that he thought might presage the end, but it usually came to nothing. One day, though, he was diagnosed with a genuine heart condition. He was on the phone in a trice. 'You'll never guess what,' he said. 'I've actually got something!'

It seemed he had a large, unruptured aneurysm, the cure for which involved clamping off his aorta and sewing in a graft to act as a bridge for his blood flow. It was a great success. He called it his bridge over troubled aorta.

Now that he has been gone for ten years I wonder even more that I might not be using however much time I have left to me to good purpose. Though what that purpose should or might be I have no real idea. Only that I am ever more conscious that anything could come along at any moment to stop me in my tracks, and turn me from a reasonably fit late-middle-aged man with a few aches and pains into a seriously old one.

A friend, fresh back from a health- and tan-giving fortnight in South Africa, discovered that no less than four of her friends had succumbed to a variety of body blows – a stroke here, a virus there, a bust hip . . .

While she was away, we had experienced something similar. One of our oldest chums had been holidaying in Somerset Maugham country and enjoying a dinner with some fellow travellers when she suddenly realised she couldn't speak properly. She had been hit by a small stroke and after a night's sleep suffered another.

At the time of writing, she is home and being treated, and doing well, as they say. But the suddenness of it has shaken both of us. A mild stroke is one thing; even two. One could get over that, and she is doing so. But not one of those Mike Tyson-sized jobs that knock you into a non-speaking, non-doing-anything wheelchair.

Apart from anything else, it buggers up so many other people's lives – not least those who have to look after you. One can sympathise with the man who was heard to announce, 'You can't believe it: my secretary's had a heart attack. Everything happens to me.'

The Bard hits the nail on the head, as usual, in the voice of the melancholy Jaques in *As You Like It*, listing the seven ages of man.

> *The sixth age shifts*
> *Into the lean and slipper'd pantaloon,*
> *With spectacles on nose and pouch on side,*
> *His youthful hose, well sav'd, a world too wide*
> *For his shrunk shank; and his big manly voice,*
> *Turning again toward childish treble, pipes*
> *And whistles in his sound. Last scene of all,*
> *That ends this strange eventful history,*
> *Is second childishness and mere oblivion;*
> *Sans teeth, sans eyes, sans taste, sans every thing.*

This might be a good moment for me to pause and consider my own state of play.

At the time of writing, I can walk without a stick; I can see pretty well without having to wear glasses, though I use them for reading; I can hear perfectly well without the need of a hearing aid; and I've still got a good head of hair.

This is nothing to be proud of. It's pure genetic luck. My father had hair all his life and there seems every chance that I will too. Like him, I look after my thatch as best I can, though I was once talked into having my greying hairs (as they were then) treated with a light dye. The barber in question was of the old school – of the kind who, when a friend of mine, aged eight, was having his hair cut at Trumper's in Curzon Street, having not uttered a word throughout, leaned forward and murmured into his ear, 'Will we be going north for the grouse this year, sir?'

The result of my adventure into rejuvenation was that I ended up prematurely orange.

I do not think I shall ever be bald or know what it is like to live *sans* thatch. Were it by mischance to happen, heaven knows what lengths I might go to in an effort to cover a bald pate. A wig would be out of the question. Wigs always look like wigs; toupées are worse. You can spot them a mile off. And the sad thing is that the people sporting them think no one has noticed.

The days of the comb-over – what was fondly known as the Bobby Charlton or, for more intellectual types, the Robert Robinson – are long past, and the current fashion for concealing baldness, premature or otherwise, is pretending it doesn't exist by shaving off the last remnants.

This would be impossible for me. In order to achieve the billiard-ball effect, one would need to have an immaculate skull, and, having once knocked myself silly on some rocks while skiing – an accident that not only very nearly killed me but required fifty-two stiches in the back of my head (without anaesthetic, I might add) – I'd look more like Frankenstein's monster than Bruce Willis.

I suppose I could add an amusing tattoo . . .

But then I'd have to grow a full goatee with moustache and risk looking like a retired science teacher turned drug manufacturer.

On the subject of crinosity, the older one gets the more hair sprouts from a variety of orifices, and with ever greater abundance. A full head of hair can appear to take years off an old geezer's life, but not if it also sprouts like an untrimmed hedge from the ears, the top of the nose, the inside of the nose and from the eyebrows, so that you look as if you have a pint of prawns stuck on your forehead.

Indeed, there are those who are convinced they are going deaf and spend a fortune on hearing aids when they would do better to have a discreet word with their hairdresser.

Thus far I have not felt the need for artificial aid when out bird-watching, or sitting in the Whispering Gallery of St Paul's Cathedral. I'll admit I sometimes can't hear everything that actors – especially American actors – say on television, but I blame them for sloppy delivery.

I did once undergo a listening test, but only because I got something through the post offering it for free. As far as I remember, it involved sitting in the dark staring at a blank screen from which little beeping noises went off in all directions. These were gradually reduced in volume and I had to press a button if I could still hear them.

One of the problems of tests like these are that they encourage undue enthusiasm, verging on plain lying. This comes partly from a genuine belief that, like a well-trained gun dog, one really can hear a sound that is inaudible to the normal human ear, and partly from a desire not to disappoint the audiologist: after all, he has gone to a lot of trouble to set the thing up and one doesn't want to make him feel he was largely wasting his time.

I suffer a similar failed sense of responsibility when at the dentist. Time and again I have sat in chairs having my face numbed, my teeth drilled and another cavity filled, wishing I could give the dentist (and the hygienist too) something really challenging to do. The best I have ever managed to offer was root canal work, and to judge from the tone of voice of all present that was pretty run-of-the-mill on the dentistry skills chart. Though I was quite gratified after it was all over (and not before time) when the dentist told me to go home and take it easy. 'After all,' he said, 'you have undergone surgery.'

The outcome of the hearing test, which I was beginning to think might show me up to have better hearing than Wolverine, proved to be disappointing. I was told that 70 per cent was about average for a man of my age.

Still, at least I have never suffered the indignity of mishearing a word in a social situation and congratulating someone on a birth when I should have been commiserating with them on a bereavement.

There's a story Willie Rushton was fond of telling about a man who went round the country giving lectures on spiritualism. Having completed his talk, he would ask his audience three questions. Had anyone there ever seen a ghost? Perhaps as many as a dozen would raise their hands. Satisfied with the answer, he would then ask if anyone had ever met a ghost. Occasionally, but not often, a couple of hands would go up. With a hint of a smile he would then enquire if anyone had ever slept with a ghost.

This would usually get a chuckle from the audience, and he would close the proceedings; but on one occasion a man at the back put his hand up and called out 'I have.'

The lecturer was astounded. 'This has never happened

before,' he said. 'Please. Come up here onto the stage and tell us what happened.'

The man, who was elderly, struggled to feet and made his way slowly on a stick through the audience and up onto the stage until he was standing next to the lecturer.

'This is quite extraordinary,' said the lecturer. 'A unique moment in my experience. Do tell us: what it is like to sleep with a ghost?'

'Oh, I'm so sorry,' said the old man. 'I thought you said goat.'

Having a Ball?

Time was – not so long ago – when the women's pages of national newspapers were a-groan with complaints from middle-aged women that their days were done. No one would look at them any more, or fancy them, or employ them, or allow them to dance at weddings.

Suddenly, women of a certain age – women journalists of a certain age, anyway – have started announcing that it's perfectly all right for them to wear skinny jeans and embarrass their children with their clothes or behaviour, and do anything they damn well want.

The great thing about being old, we are frequently told in style and women's pages, is that Baby Boomers don't care what people think about them any more – the suggestion being that however unconfident you may have been when young, all that has now vanished, and because you are getting on a bit and people wouldn't want to be seen putting a silver-haired person in their place, she or he can behave as badly as they like.

Is any of this remotely true, or is this something that has

been dreamed up by newspaper editors in an attempt to pull in more elderly readers?

There was a feature in *The Times* recently about how deeply unconfident the splendidly septuagenarian Dame Helen Mirren was as a young woman, and how age has helped her overcome her self-doubt. Life is getting better all the time, she is quoted as saying. The Boomers are having a ball at seventy.

While I am only too delighted to know how happy Dame Helen is with herself these days, I can't help thinking that if you are as successful and rich and good looking as she is, you have little reason to be otherwise.

It would seem that one of the main reasons she gave the interview was because she is an ambassador for the cosmetics giant L'Oréal Paris ('Because you're worth it'), which has just hitched up with the Prince's Trust to help give young people self-confidence. Nothing wrong with that. But while young women nowadays seem to me to be more self-confident than they ever were when I was as young, the women I meet who are my age now seem every bit as unconfident as I am. Indeed, it's the really successful ones who seem the least confident: in everyday life, anyway.

It goes without saying that when it comes to professions, women are every bit as assured as men, but few can claim to be constantly on top of things when coping with tricky families, or organising social activities, or even just going shopping.

And there's no reason why, because newspapers like to fill their magazines and supplements and lifestyle pages with generalisations and all-round guff about the pleasures of growing old, based on a handful of celebrities, women born with a naturally modest, reserved and unassuming nature should be chivvied into feeling they are missing out on something.

Seventy is not the new fifty; it's the new seventy. And if Joanna Lumley adores being seventy because, she says, at seventy we lose our fear, who am I to gainsay her? Helen Mirren at seventy is welcome to feel as free and liberated as she wants, and to be what she wants to be. Others of their ilk may well be having a ball and doing what the hell they like, wearing short skirts, backpacking in Thailand and generally behaving like superannuated gappers, and for all I know they may be as happy as clams at high water.

Or they may not. Women like them could just be saying these things simply because somebody from a newspaper has rung up their agent and asked for a quote, and because no actress, however distinguished, wants to risk anyone thinking they might be over the hill and therefore unemployable, they say what they think readers want to hear.

It's entirely understandable. There was a time when the roles for women over forty were decidedly thin on the ground. This is no longer the case.

The great octogenarian Dame Judi Dench never stops working, nor do Dames Penelope Keith, Eileen Atkins, Penelope Wilton and Joan Collins, or Alison Steadman, or Patricia Hodge, or ... I could go on for the rest of the page.

I feel quite sure they are all utterly self-confident and as busy as beavers, but are the millions of women of about the same age who don't have glamorous, well-paid jobs – or indeed have no job at all – and some of whom live in horrible homes and have horrible jobs and horrible husbands and generally horrible lives? Or even just humdrum lives. They're all Baby Boomers, like Miss Lumley and Dame Helen, but how many of them have forgotten what it is like to be fearful and couldn't give a toss what anyone thinks of them, and are having a ball, and reading endless newspaper articles that have them worrying why they aren't?

Women who suddenly start worrying that they might be getting old should take courage from the life of Dorothy Parker. One of the brightest and funniest of the gang that met regularly at the Algonquin Hotel in New York in the twenties, she and her friends created a style which, in the words of her biographer John Keats, 'called for one to go through life armed with a wry, hard suspicion; to be always ready to acknowledge excellence, but equally ready to express an informed contempt for all that was in any way bogus – meanwhile being just as ready to have a damned good time at every opportunity'.

'Promise me,' she said to all those who came to interview her on her seventieth birthday, 'promise me I won't get old.'

She died three years later. Her tiny body may have failed her towards the end, but her mind remained as fresh and sharp as ever – as did her wit. 'It stayed in no place,' wrote her friend Lillian Hellman, 'and was of no time ... She was part of nothing and nobody except herself.'

Whale Steak Memories

Twenty years ago I wrote a book called *A Nightingale Sang in Fernhurst Road*. It was about a twelve-year-old boy in leafy, Home Counties commuterland in 1945.

Having spent the entire war alone with his mother, his life is thrown into confusion when his father, whom he hardly knows, returns from long service in the Middle East.

I had intended it to be autobiographical. However, there were certain differences between my life and that of my young hero that meant I had to make a few changes.

My father was indeed away during the war – in the Home Counties, mainly – and for some of that time I was alone with my mother. Until 1944, that is, when my brother was a small baby and my father, by then thirty-eight, was invalided out of the army.

As far as I know, his reappearance in our lives went unnoticed by me, and at no time had my mother felt the need to seek solace in the arms of a man I knew only as 'uncle'.

The local prep school I described bore a striking resemblance to the one I attended. The headmaster was equally obsessed with physical courage, the junior masters were similarly ill-equipped to teach, and the school boxing competition was every bit as bloody as I portrayed it.

However, I did not in fact set foot in the school in the way described, for the simple reason that in 1945 I was only six. The reason my hero is twice as old is because I told the story as if it were a diary written by him, and there was no way a six-year-old could write something good enough to be published and sold for £12.99.

As a result of these adjustments to my real life, a number of the events I described were not entirely accurate.

What am I talking about? Not entirely accurate? However much I may try to kid myself, most of my stories were either a quarter true and three-quarters lightly burnished, or told to me by other people, or wholly invented.

In the bookshops the title was categorised, rightly, as light fiction.

And yet, all the way through writing it, I felt sure it was a pretty accurate account of my early childhood.

The truth is that the episodes themselves are reasonably accurate – merely rearranged to fit the situation.

As Eric Morecambe told André Previn, when having played his version of the Grieg Piano Concerto the great man accused him of playing all the wrong notes, 'I'm playing all the right notes, but not necessarily in the right order.'

All of which is nothing more than a flowery prelude to the moment when I was telling Tug and Ludo about the sort of food we used to eat during the war. Like sausages that tasted of sawdust. When Tug contested the truth of this assertion, I pointed out that in those days people ate a lot of things they wouldn't normally have eaten and that really weren't at all nice.

'Such as?' said Ludo.

'Such as snoek,' I said.

'Snook? Wasn't he a cartoon character?'

'I know people did weird things in those days, but I don't think anyone would have thought of getting laughs out of a snake mackerel.'

They stared at me.

Tug pulled a face. '*Snake?*'

'It's a fish,' I said. 'A very long fish and a very boney one which you find only in the southern hemisphere: South Africa, South America and so on. It was also a very nasty fish. But a lot of people ate it, and liked it. It was cheap, and there wasn't much else around. Any that was left over after the war was sold as tinned cat food.'

She didn't seem as surprised as I had expected. But then I told her that a lot of people ate horse meat, mainly because it wasn't rationed: you just had to queue up for it. It had a slightly sweet taste and the fat was very yellow.

'Yuck.'

While I had her on the gastronomic ropes, I threw in whale meat for good measure.

'That's awful,' she said. 'I thought whales were a protected species.'

'Not during the war. Anything was better than nothing. Except, perhaps, whale meat. It was inedible. But we still had whale steak for Sunday lunch. Quite often, actually.'

Hang on a second. What was I talking about? No one could accuse me of selling the young short on useful information, but there are limits, and I suddenly got the feeling I was fast drifting into fantasy.

One of the dangers of people of my age reminiscing about the war, and their early childhood in general, is that a lot of what they trot out is, although they probably don't realise it, based on stuff they'd once been told by their parents and grandparents. Having heard the story a few times, they are convinced they had personal experience of rationing of more or less every basic form of food, of whale meat cooked in all sorts of imaginative ways, of an absence of bananas, and of all-round deprivation.

Did sausages really taste like sawdust? Or did I read somewhere that somebody said they tasted like sawdust? Or had I just made it up to add extra colour to the story? The clearer the picture we have in our minds of people and places and events in our personal histories, the more blurred and unreliable they become.

I am convinced – certainly I have convinced myself – that when I was a schoolboy it snowed every year between Christmas and New Year: not just a light dusting of the kind we are used to now, but heavily enough that the steep field beyond the wood next to us was perfect for tobogganing; and I and my friends, and often their parents, would spend days hurtling down on a variety of sledges – many of them knocked together by fathers in garden sheds – before hauling them to the top and trying to see how near we could get to the stream at the bottom without actually going in.

Looking through the meteorological report for 1945 to 1955, I see that the winter of 1946–7 was one of the coldest on record (though it didn't actually snow until January 21st, when we would all have been back at school); and that, apart from a heavy fall of snow over the south of England in April 1950, the winters appeared to have been largely wet, with little snow to speak of.

Well, you could have fooled me. I certainly seem to have fooled myself.

And now there I was pontificating on the culinary merits of the whale. Did whale meat ever darken our doors? And, if so, did I ever taste any? It is certainly not something that has stuck in my mind, or indeed in my throat. Which, of course, isn't to say that seventy years ago I might not have noticed.

But why spoil a good story? Writers lie all the time, so what harm could one more small white one do?

'What did it taste like?'

'A bit like shark,' I said firmly.

'Gosh,' she said, scribbling hard into her notebook. 'That's really interesting. What does shark taste like?'

'It's rather like conger eel.'

What? I mean, do *you* know what it tastes like? I could have said it's a bit like chicken. But that would have been such a boring answer to a question that demanded one that was interesting; exotic, even.

I can't pretend I'm happy at the idea of fibbing to my grand-children, but that's writers for you.

Irritable Vowel Syndrome

In 1993 Michael Douglas starred in a film called *Falling Down*. It was about a man, recently laid off from his job in the defence industry, who gets stuck in the mother and father of a traffic jam and, late for his daughter's birthday party, gets out of his car and walks.

Confronted by humiliations at every turn (a shopkeeper refuses to give him change for the telephone; a fast-food joint won't serve him breakfast because he is three minutes late and they're only taking lunch orders; a pair of elderly golf-club members pepper him with balls when he tries to cross the course), he gradually loses the plot. Sadness turns to madness and, from being a frustrated victim of a hostile world, he becomes a gun-toting menace to all who cross his path.

The older I get, the more I sympathise with him. I have long pictured myself in old age as a benevolent, passive figure, for whom confrontation is a distant memory, resigned to whatever modern life might throw at me. At seventy-eight, I find I am quite the opposite. I am told that only this summer a friend of mine spotted this white-haired, red-faced man in an elderly VW Golf in the high street of one of our quieter seaside towns, gesticulating with his arms and yelling through the windscreen at a little old lady driver dithering around in the middle of the road in a hopeless attempt to find a parking space: 'For God's sake make up your mind: if you're going to park, PARK!'

I presume there was someone at the wheel. Old ladies tend, like all of us, to grow smaller with age, and it is not unusual in seaside towns in England to find oneself behind a small car in which there appears to be no one at the wheel. The suspicion that the car might somehow be driving itself would seem to be justified, since the vehicle is moving not only at a snail's pace but unfortunately not with a snail's sense of direction, or concentration. The right indicator may be flashing, but that is no proof that the car is going to move to the right. Indeed, it may well do the very opposite. You just have to hope that, having finally made up its mind, it's not then going to try to park.

The older one gets, the trickier parking becomes, mainly because, one's back having stiffened up, it's a hell of job to twist round in one's seat in order to reverse, so one has to resort to doing it using just the rear-view mirror, so one never quite knows where one is going to be at any given moment. Or, in some cases, where one was meant to be in the first place.

So I do sympathise with whoever it was who was seen shouting at the little old lady (if indeed there was one). I suppose it's possible it could have been me. I did once drive a Golf when on holiday, and I am not alone in finding other drivers extremely indecisive at times; my hair is certainly on the white side, but I don't think anyone could describe my face as red. Sun-tanned, maybe.

And I have to admit I do suffer from the occasional attack of IVS – Irritable Vowel Syndrome. This is usually, though not always, associated with being at the wheel of a car. At my age time could be running out, and I am not prepared to waste a nanosecond of it waiting at a traffic light while the driver in front of me (or, in many cases, several cars ahead) wakes up to the fact that the lights have changed, engages an appropriate gear, moves slowly forward looking to right and left, even though his (or her) light is clearly showing green, then, at the very last minute, indicates that he (or she) wishes to turn right across the oncoming traffic, and stops.

Equally irritating are those who leave huge gaps, so that when the lights are green they do not allow sufficient time for everyone who should be able to cross to do so.

Worst of all are the ones who dither when approaching an easy green light, then speed up just as the lights are changing, leaving me standing. Or more worryingly, making a desperately desperate dash on a red light.

As for trying to negotiate one's way through the morning and evening rush hour cyclists ... don't get me started.

Mind you, I doubt I am alone in feeling deeply disgruntled at being forced to sit in a single-line traffic jam in Lower Thames Street (between two builders' lorries, as like as not), while a single cyclist sails merrily past in one of the ex-mayor's inspired cycle lanes

There are various disadvantages to shouting in cars, one of which is the possibility of a stroke or heart failure. Indeed, I understand from long and serious research on the internet that general rattiness can itself be a symptom of heart disease and a pending cardiac arrest. The other downside is that it upsets the other people in the car, and to anyone who happens to glance across while you are in mid-bellow, you are an ocean-going arse.

It is a common condition among older drivers – the kind who were taught to double declutch and signal out of the window whenever they were planning to turn or to invite the driver behind to overtake, and who, despite now driving cars equipped with every imaginable mod con, still do – to believe that most people on the roads these days should not be. Shouting and gesticulating are only two of the many techniques deployed to express their views.

Muttering is a favourite with many. An elderly woman friend used to be given a lift to her Women's Institute meetings by a man who looked, spoke and behaved like a Central Casting colonel (retired). He muttered most of the way, and seemed convinced that anyone who did anything on a road must be at best a road hog and at worst a danger to life, limb and law-abiding roadmanship.

A car had only to pull out of a turning two hundred yards ahead and she could hear him muttering, 'Now what's *this* b.f. up to?'

Others take matters into their hands in no uncertain terms, sometimes at risk to themselves and others. I remember a friend at school telling me about his grandfather and how he dealt with drivers who dithered along on empty roads, holding him up, even if he was not in a particular hurry. If the heavy hand on the horn didn't achieve the required result, he would come up close behind the driver and nudge him gently with his bumper. Ah, bumpers. Those were the days.

You might not credit it from the above, but I have rather a fondness, if not sympathy, for people much older than myself – particularly old ladies – who have driving licences dating almost from before the introduction of the compulsory driving test. They're the ones who tend to sit with their bosoms practically resting on the steering wheel, who do a lot of revving up between gear changes (usually when they fail to locate the gear they were looking for), and arrive next to the pavement more by luck than by judgement.

I had an elderly aunt who contrived to find herself not only driving into someone's front garden but into their sitting room, and a friend of mine had a venerable godmother in Italy who drove a Fiat so small that whenever he went anywhere with her he had to open the canvas sun roof and travel with the top of his head sticking out.

For some reason she had never learned how to reverse, so whenever they went shopping she would drive the whole length of the town in one direction, take a roundabout at the far end and drive all the way back before being in a suitable position to park.

Eccentricity, as demonstrated by the very old, is rather a thing of the past and in its extreme form will, as likely as not, be diagnosed as mild dementia, with the person in question being deemed incapable of driving and having their licence revoked.

Time was when it was not unusual for someone like my late mother-in-law to climb into her car after a morning's shopping and wonder why the controls weren't where they were meant to be, only to realise she had got into the back seat.

At least she was stationary when she discovered her mistake. An old friend of mine was in the passenger seat of his elderly mother's car when he suggested that she was not driving quite as carefully as she might.

'Oh,' she said. 'Am *I* driving?'

Payback Time

My father had ambitions for me to make a career in the law. He hoped that I would be called to the Bar, practise for a while, then join a big firm like Shell, work my way up the ladder in the legal department, retire in my early sixties with a handsome pension, and enjoy a long and happy old age, gardening, playing golf and taking cruises.

I did have a job for a while during the sixties, as an advertising copywriter in a variety of West End ad agencies. I left the last one when it closed and I was made redundant, and I found myself with two months' salary, unemployed and, to all intents and purposes, unemployable.

Luckily, it was possible in those days to eke out a modest living as a freelance journalist for papers like *The Sunday Times*, for whom I wrote travel pieces and humorous bits and bobs in the Look pages. Since all my travelling was done at the expense of national tourist offices, airlines and PR companies, a tin of baked beans in the larder was all I needed by way of a fallback. Luckily, too, I was single for the first few years of this haphazard existence, so I did not feel a pressing need to get another job. And I never have.

If I had, I could hardly be worse off now on a company pension than I am with the ludicrously Lilliputian reward that dribbles into my bank account every month from my juicy-sounding annuity. My father's plan does not, on reflection, sound quite as humdrum as I had imagined at the time.

On the other hand, I have never had to commute, or attend office parties, or wear a suit and tie every day, or remember to dress down on Fridays, or to stand by the water cooler discussing the previous evening's episode of *Celebrity Masterchef*.

For forty-seven years, going on forty-eight, I have been my own man, and happy with that. But what of retirement and those long, carefree days in well-earned clover?

The answer is that I can whistle for it. It's never going to happen. For countless thousands of self-employees, this, as a fellow freelance hack once put it, is payback time. A life of leisure is not for us. If anything, we can look forward to working even harder than ever.

What's more, we expect to be doing so until the day we drop off the twig. Not just because we have to, but because we wouldn't know what to do with our time otherwise.

By the age of ninety-three, P. G. Wodehouse had written seventy-one novels, twenty-four collections of short stories, forty-two plays and musicals, and three autobiographies. And what he was doing in hospital in February 1975 the day before he died? Working on a new novel, *Sunset at Blandings*. What else?

Whether it was he who said it, or his biographer or

someone else altogether, the fact is that Wodehouse wrote mainly to please himself. It was an occupation that he loved more than any other.

In 1927 his wife Ethel bought a house in Norfolk Street (now Dunraven Street) in Mayfair because she felt it was time her husband – famously reclusive – should enjoy a more sociable existence. To this end she threw parties to which she invited friends, fellow writers and the kind of people she felt he might like to know and with whom he would feel comfortable.

She was sadly mistaken. While her guests partied in the main reception rooms, her husband remained upstairs in his study, writing.

The playwright Frederick Lonsdale was invited to one such soirée in Norfolk Street with one of his daughters. He rang the doorbell and was surprised when it was opened by Plum himself.

'Oh, please don't come in,' said his old friend. 'You'll absolutely hate it.' And he slammed the door in Lonsdale's face.

Dr Johnson, who always had something to say about just about everything (I have always thought of him as the original pub bore), declared on the subject of authorship: 'No man but a blockhead ever wrote, except for money.'

He was wrong about that, as he was about so many things. Writers love nothing better than the actual business of sitting down and writing. They will give interviews if asked, and perform at literary festivals, and appear on local radio somewhere between the weather forecasts and the traffic announcements, but these are mere distractions. Even the rigmarole leading towards and around publication itself can be quite irksome compared with the pleasure getting the words down on the page.

It doesn't get any easier the older one gets, but the pleasure, if anything, increases.

Anthony Powell once compared writing fiction with daydreaming: faces, voices, incidents, lines of poetry, pictures, jokes, long since buried in the sludge of memory, suddenly emerge, as if fresh minted, ready for immediate use.

'I love writing,' says John le Carré in his memoir, *The Pigeon Tunnel*, written in the Swiss chalet which he built with the profits from *The Spy Who Came in from the Cold*. 'I love doing what I'm doing at this moment, scribbling away like a man in hiding at a poky desk on a black-clouded early morning in May, with the mountain rain scuttling down the window and no excuse for tramping down to the railway station under an umbrella because the *International New York Times* doesn't arrive till lunchtime.'

He also loves 'writing on the hoof, in notebooks on walks, in trains and cafés, then scurrying home to pick over my booty'.

At the time of publishing his memoir, le Carré was eighty-five, with twenty-two hugely successful novels under his belt, in addition to countless newspaper and magazine articles.

All of us who have been doing what we love for most of our lives can count ourselves lucky; but so can those who have worked hard at demanding jobs for thirty years or more, and retired to do what they love and have waited all those years to do.

Several of my friends have done exactly that. Two gave up their day jobs – one in publishing, the other in the law – to become successful painters. A third – another publisher – is a distinguished sculptor. A fourth, once a solicitor in a large London firm, is writing a thesis on macroeconomics at his old university.

'I worked all those years in order that I could do what I'm doing now,' he said.

Perhaps one's greatest fear as one heads towards the exit is of no longer being wanted; of being overtaken by younger names and faces and landing on the scrap heap. The well-worn phrase 'every dog has his day' hangs over one's head like a balloon in a bad cartoon. One should, I suppose, be grateful to have had a day at all, but, as a writer, one is left with a strong sense that one is going to be remembered for one book and one book only. Never mind that one's favourite is barely mentioned in the obituaries, let alone the two dozen others that were admired and sold well. The subheading beneath one's name will be the one that pins your reputation for all time.

Even the great le Carré has his misgivings. 'If you're ever lucky enough to score an early success as a writer,' he says in *The Pigeon Tunnel*, 'for the rest of your life there's a before-the-fall and an after-the-fall. You look back at the books you wrote before the spotlight picked you out and they read like the books of your innocence; and the books after it, in your low moments, like the strivings of a man on trial.'

Writers are not alone in having such thoughts. It must be even more worrying for actors who were once playing Prospero at Stratford and are now pathetically thankful for a couple of lines in a *Harry Potter* film.

I remember a moment in a West End farce many years ago

41

in which the final scene featured an elderly man wearing, for some reason that I cannot now remember, nothing but bondage gear. He didn't have any lines, or anything to do except to stand there looking embarrassed and thoroughly pathetic. The audience almost fell out of their seats laughing.

Had this man once been compared with Olivier and Gielgud, I wondered.

Did his cuttings files contain a glowing review by Harold Hobson of his magnificent Lear? How the mighty are fallen, I thought.

But perhaps not. Perhaps his career had been filled with small character parts that had set countless audiences on a roar, and that evening he was merely doing what he had always done and always loved doing and would continue to do as long as he was asked to.

Some years ago I interviewed the actress Judy Campbell. Tall, elegant, with a swan-like neck and a smoky singing voice, for more than sixty years she was one of Britain's best-loved boulevard actresses. She was Noël Coward's leading lady in *Blithe Spirit*, *This Happy Breed* and *Present Laughter*, and at the age of eighty-five appeared on stage at the King's Head and Jermyn Street Theatres in a nostalgic piece called *Where Are the Songs We Sang?* She was most famous for being the first actress to sing 'A Nightingale Sang in Berkeley Square' in a revue called *New Faces* at the Comedy Theatre in 1941.

She spoke of her career, of the people she had known and the plays she had acted in, and concluded, 'I just know that all the obituaries will talk about nothing but that blooming nightingale.'

And, guess what: they all did.

I think she would have been pleased. Who wouldn't want to be remembered, if only for one achievement? Like so many for whom retirement in old age is unthinkable, Judy was a perfect example of one who took to heart the words of Winston Churchill: KBO – Keep Buggering On.

Hi, Christopher

The doctor I see on a regular basis is young, tall, charming, interested in everything I have to say about myself and my condition (whatever that may be at the time), and extremely friendly. Oh, and – I almost forgot to mention it – a woman.

At another time and in different circumstances, I might have chatted with her for a while about this and that and suggested meeting later for a drink or a spot of dinner. I see no hint in her eyes or mouth that such a thought might ever have crossed her mind, but it still grieves me when she pops her head round her door and calls out my name, and as I enter her office enquires politely, 'How are you, Mr Matthew?'

At that moment my shoulders sag, my knees ache, my white hair grows whiter, and there is not a scintilla of doubt in my mind that I am just another OAP patient.

The other day, I could contain myself no longer.

'Oh dear,' I said as I took my seat next to her desk. 'I do wish you didn't have to call me Mr Matthew. It makes me feel so old.'

She smiled. 'How's the back?' she said.

When Ludo asked me whether I enjoyed being called

Christopher by younger people, I said, truthfully, that it depended who was doing the calling.

There are two types for whom the words 'hackles' and 'rise' spring to mind: one, those who do it, like they did to my mother in hospital, because they feel it puts a subject at his or her ease; and two, those who are trying to sell me something, have found my name on some list somewhere, and because my address or past purchasing performance or whatever fits the profile of the perfect customer, they feel entitled to treat me as if I were not only one already, but one of the best and of many years' standing.

At the same time, of course, if it is some form of paid work they are hoping to sell me, the immediate use of my Christian name does suggest that, since I am reasonably fit and blessed with my marbles, I might still be employable. I have no real idea in what capacity. I mean, I can't imagine anyone inviting me to be the non-executive chairman of Cazenove's; nor do I live in hope of being invited to take over as Private Secretary to the Duke of Edinburgh. But there must be something useful I can do with the last years of my life.

I would dearly like my obituary in the local church magazine to record that I had been somebody unusual or done something interesting in the course of my life: the oldest man to swim single-handed across Hackney Baths, perhaps; or the winner of *Strictly Come Dancing* with my once-iconic rendering of the twist; or that I'd converted Carol Ann Duffy to the joys of comic verse.

'Dream on,' said Mrs Matthew.

And then I read, only the other day, about a man called Joe Bartley, an ex-serviceman from Paignton in Devon. Having lost his wife, and being bored out of his skull, he put an ad in a local paper offering his services – to clean, garden or do a spot of DIY. He received offers from all over the world, notably from the Cantina Bar and Kitchen just down the road, and at the age of eighty-nine started work as a waiter. A steady-handed one, I hope.

Inspired, I began to pen a lively ad for insertion in the *Kensington and Chelsea Times* when out of blue appeared a *deus ex machina* in the shape of an e-mail from a company called Career Acclaimed!

'Hi, Christopher,' it began. 'Your Personalized Job Matches.'

Personalized! How has this come about? How do they know enough about me to feel confident that every job in the list that follows would be right up my street? And if they do, presumably they must also know my age. Are they suggesting that British Airways and others are crying out for seventy-eight-year-old airline baggage co-ordinators at £15 an hour? If I know anything about watching others (i.e., members of my family) handling baggage in a departure area, there inevitably comes a moment when I have to step in and lend a hand, and with my back as stiff as it is, that could be terminal. (Sorry, no joke intended.)

While on the subject of travel, being a member of an airline cabin crew would appear to be thought of as marginally less responsible than baggage handling, paying as it does a mere £10.85 an hour. On the other hand, I have always felt that I am not familiar with quite as many foreign lands and their cultures as I would like, and the opportunity to spend time in airports in places like Delhi and Beijing and Ulaanbaatar could give me a taste of countries that I could never otherwise afford to visit.

Life as a parking attendant at £11 an hour could be ideal, since in my experience this largely involves sitting in a booth, watching cars drive in and out, and occasionally having to inform drivers that, whatever they may suspect to the contrary, the car park is full.

A late career as a receptionist at £19,750 a year could suit someone of my age who is good at getting on with strangers, has telephonic skills and a good memory (to remind visitors to hand in their passes), and needs to remain seated for long periods. I am also quite tempted by the thought of becoming a professional driver at £30,624, provided the passengers have a taste for fruity language and explosions of road rage compared with which Basil Fawlty would seem as mild and well-mannered as the Katie Johnson character in *The Ladykillers*.

The only other job on the list that might appeal to someone of my age is undertaker. The money's good (forty-two grand a year) and, in the event of one's sudden demise, one could not hope to find oneself in more convenient hands.

Postscript: It would seem that I am not alone in looking around for a new career. The former Page 3 girl Katie Price is, if a recent interview with Lynn Barber in *The Sunday Times* is to be believed, casting around for a fresh start which she hopes will be of benefit to one and all. She is going to train as a paramedic. Good on her.

'I've seen them on TV,' she said, 'and some of them are quite old. I'd love to be a paramedic, dashing in and saving lives.'

Me, too. With Katie Price, preferably.

'Keep dreaming,' said Mrs Matthew.

The Younger Model

In Deborah Moggach's novel *Something to Hide*, a sad, single, sixty-something woman called Petra falls in love with an old mate called Jeremy on a visit from abroad. He suggests they find somewhere to eat: 'I don't want any of this gastro bollocks. I want somewhere with tired old waiters with stains on their jackets, and tinned grapefruit for starters . . . and melba toast.'

They stumble on just such a restaurant, called Frederico's: the menu hasn't been changed for decades, nor have the gingham curtains, nor, very possibly, has the waiter. The two of them sit there, as if in a gastronomic time warp, reminiscing about the days of Mateus Rosé and Hirondelle, fondue sets, Cliff Michelmore and the Triumph Stag, and conclude that men who run off with younger women must be mad and sad. It must be so lonely, talking about bands they've never heard of and trends they don't understand, and, worst of all, trying to look as if they're interested. And then the woman would want to have babies.

'And the poor bastard has to pretend that he does too,' says Jeremy.

'And lo and behold – he's pushing a double buggy around Aldi with two squalling brats and his dodgy knee's playing up and he's thinking is it really worth it, just for a firm young body with firm young breasts.'

Had the waiter not arrived at that moment with more bread sticks, Deborah's retro pair might have gone on to reflect that firm young breasts become a lot less firm and a lot less youthful; that small children grow up to be teenagers while school fees rocket to Shard-like heights; his prostate starts to play up and his libido goes down; and, before you can say knife, she finds herself nursing an elderly geezer who is wondering why he went to all that trouble to acquire a Mark Two wife when he could have stayed with the first and they could have grown old together.

Mind you, when I was young and single and unlucky in love, there was a widely held theory that girls went for the older man. It didn't work for me, but there must have been countless thousands who fell for it, never imagining that the older man, who had once seemed so suave and wise and witty, would turn out to be quite that old, or quite so soon.

It really didn't take the genius of Shakespeare to remind us that summer's lease hath all too short a date . . .

Someone I know (let's call him Charles) married, for the second time, a lovely girl twenty years his junior. Being able, at the age of fifty, to appear at his friends' dinner parties with a beautiful twenty-eight-year-old on his arm and introduce her to his fellow guests with 'I don't believe you know my wife . . .' did no end of wonders for his self-esteem.

Some years later, now with a growing family, he met an old friend he hadn't seen for years who said, with perhaps a hint of envy, 'I'm told you have a very young wife.'

'Indeed,' said Charles.

'How old is she?'

'She's thirty-nine.'

'Oh,' said the man. 'Not *that* young, then.'

The other day I fell into conversation with a taxi driver, who informed me that for some years he had worked as a private chauffeur to a very rich man, but that the job had ended badly. Not for him, but for his employer, who had dropped dead at the age of sixty-five.

I remarked that sixty-five was no age.

'He had just married a girl forty years younger than himself. I think that may have had something to do with it.'

I couldn't resist it. It was an old story, but it was a tedious journey in the middle of the rush hour.

'Have you heard the one about the older man who married someone way younger than himself? A friend told him, "Do take care. This could be dangerous."

'The man shrugged, "Well," he said, "if she dies, she dies."'

'Nice one,' said the driver.

However great the setbacks and disappointments on both sides, you will never persuade a man, be he ever so silver-haired and sere, that he has not still got what it takes with pretty girls – or girls of any kind.

It is one nature's cruellest tricks to inform you in no uncertain terms that you are way beyond your sell-by date, and yet allow you to believe quite the opposite.

In his splendid book on middle age – *A Shed of One's Own* – Marcus Berkmann depicts a man 'in his seventies or eighties, shuffling along the pavement ... In his imagination he is striding at a healthy pace, fast enough to overtake the beautiful young woman ahead of him with the exquisite buttocks.'

Ah, well, a beautiful young woman glimpsed in the street will always stir a man's heart, whatever his age, though sadly not always his limbs. For a brief and happy moment or two, even the most clapped-out among us can almost believe that our days are not done and that romance could once more be in the air.

The likelihood of a seventy-something-year-old being able to keep up with a fit young woman a third his age is, of course, as absurd as thinking that he might actually get near enough to exchange a smile or a warm greeting, but there's no harm in dreaming.

And such fleeting moments can never be more than dreams, because it is a truth universally acknowledged that old people are invisible to the young.

The story goes that George Melly and Ronnie Scott were standing chatting outside Ronnie's club in Soho when they noticed two pretty girls coming towards them along the pavement. The two old jazzers treated them to their warmest and most welcoming smiles. The girls walked on by.

'I don't think they fancied us, Ron.'

'They never even saw us, George.'

Mens Sana in Corpore Arthritico

I was going through my wardrobe recently, calculating that I probably had enough shirts and socks to see me out, but that I'd possibly have to think about some new underpants, when I came across a plastic bag that I didn't recognise. Inside was a pair of tracksuit bottoms in light grey, size 36 regular.

Never having knowingly worn any such garment, and Mrs Matthew claiming no knowledge of its provenance, I spent the rest of the day wondering how on earth such an unlikely object could have infiltrated my wardrobe. The property of a previous owner, perhaps, left behind in a moment of carelessness? Or perhaps on purpose?

It was a few days later that I remembered that some years ago I had come up with a cunning plan for tackling the growing stiffness in my back and left thigh: the one the result of two hip-replacement operations on the same side, the other the result of a childhood riding accident.

If an Australian study is to be believed, exercise is a far better cure for backache than anti-inflammatory pills. So, of course, is jumping off a tall building, but one feels one ought to go along with these things, so I had started investigating possible exercises that might suit a man of my age – and of my limited interest in the keep-fit industry.

I can't remember now who it was who recommended I join a feng shui class, but ... no, hang on: feng shui is something else, to do with front doors. Or is it a delicacy I once ordered from the local Chinese takeaway? I meant t'ai chi. That exercise thing elderly Chinese do in large groups, very early in the morning and very slowly.

I had considered other possibilities. Mrs Matthew is a big fan of yoga and has been doing it for years – evidently to great effect. With her encouragement I joined her small class one day and came away realising a) that I am incapable of breathing in and out at the same time as making particular movements, b) that it's embarrassing to be lying next to one's spouse, incapable of the simplest manoeuvre in any direction and c) that the only bit I really enjoyed was at the very end, lying flat out with a blanket over me and falling fast asleep.

Someone else not much younger than me had mentioned that she had joined a pilates class and had never felt better, so I looked it up online. It said that it is suitable for all ages and fitness levels. That's what it said, but looking at the many pictures of people in action, there wasn't a single grey hair in sight. Not one of the practitioners looked a nanosecond over thirty, and all were in positions that people of my age can only dream of.

T'ai chi seemed – from what I could glean from films of elderly Chinese citizens moving gracefully through a series of simple movements in the Beijing smog, any of which I felt

I could manage and did not involve being in anything other than the standing position – to be right up my street, and I went along to my nearest council sports centre to make enquiries.

My first disappointment was to discover that my teacher would be not a wizened Chinese sage or a beautiful young female, but a middle-aged Londoner whose cockney tones spoke more of a boxing coach than a t'ai chi master. Even so, I might have gone ahead with it, had the classes not happened to take place on an inconvenient evening.

I'm not quite sure why I went to the length of buying the tracksuit bottoms – possibly because I saw them on sale somewhere. Clearly, that was as far as I got, but now I'm beginning to wonder if I was wrong to dismiss the chance of enjoying – if that's the right word – a harmless and sociable activity once a week that is obviously beneficial, otherwise Chinese pensioners would not be out in their thousands every morning practising it.

I looked it up again on the internet the other day. 'The gentle flowing movements in t'ai chi promote relaxation, stress relief and conscious awareness of the present moment. T'ai chi may help reduce stress, depression and anxiety, improve your balance and co-ordination, lower your blood pressure and promote better sleep, *among other benefits*.'

It's got to be a no-brainer.

Anyway, I took my first step into one of the great mysteries of the Orient by slipping into the aforesaid trousers; and very silly I looked in them too. Like the back end of a pantomime horse during a rehearsal break. I hadn't got round to buying a suitable pair of lightweight slippers, but I took off my brogues and socks and looked up a few simple moves of the sort recommended for beginners.

I began with what I seem to remember was called White Stork Spreads Wings. Or was it Carry Tiger to Mountain? I forget now. Anyway, it couldn't have been easier and I looked forward to a sense of inner peace.

What I got, in fact, was a sharp pain in my lower back. The physiotherapy is definitely helping, and I've put the tracksuit bottoms back in the wardrobe, just in case.

Mind you, I'm really beginning to wonder if taking up any form of exercise late in life if you have not been in the swing of it for some years before is really as beneficial as the so-called experts would have one believe.

No one of any age who has ever passed me in the park in full running regalia (pants *on top of* tights?) looks totally happy or really all that well; indeed, the elderly look at best as if they are accommodating a large artichoke, at worst as if they are suffering the cruellest excesses of the Spanish Inquisition.

The internet is of no help, dishing out contradictory judgements on the benefits of jogging in old age – and by old age, they are talking about anyone over fifty-five.

'Jogging keeps you young,' I read in one entry; this is immediately followed by a list of things that are not only guaranteed to make you feel even older, but could well have you hospitalised before you have run half a mile.

These include loss of ability to sweat and decreasing sense of thirst, leading to major dehydration before you even begin to realise you are thirsty; and the exacerbation of back and neck pain, which can be further exacerbated by jogging downhill. This must be particularly bad news for elderly jog-gers living in the Lake District.

Call me a fitness denier, but I'm beginning to wonder if there comes a time in one's life when one has better things to do with one's remaining years than worrying about keeping one's weight down, one's cholesterol low and one's heart rate slow. I didn't get to the age I am today by fussing about my health.

Nor did P. G. Wodehouse, who would get up every morn-ing at half-past seven, step out onto the porch and perform his 'daily dozen' – a series of simple exercises he had stuck to every day since 1920 (touching his toes, rotating his trunk, stretching his back, etc.) before settling down to his regular breakfast of toast and honey and tea with a 'breakfast book' by a good mystery writer such as Rex Stout or Ngaio Marsh.

If anyone can come up with a more agreeable way of keep-ing fit as a flea into one's tenth decade, I'd like to hear about it.

Winter of Discontent

'One of the most irritating things about getting old,' said a woman friend at Sunday lunch over a particularly nice piece of pork belly, 'is not having any idea of how much longer one has got. Take the case of our car, for example. We don't need to replace it immediately, but we'll have to one day. Supposing we left it for a year or two and then got a new one, only to discover that we'd only got a few more months to live. I mean, that would be really annoying. Same problem with George's dinner jacket.

'He's seventy-eight now. His old one's practically falling to bits, but what would be the point of getting a new one if he isn't going to get decent use out of it?'

I bit down on a rather hard piece of crackling. 'Hm,' I said.

Ludo, aged thirteen and a half, happened to overhear me relating this to Mrs Matthew.

'I wouldn't want to know how long I'm going to live,' he said. 'If I did, I'd waste far too much time counting down the months and days. A bit like people waiting for midnight on

New Year's Eve. I'd much rather it came as a surprise. I like surprises.'

To the young, death is as inconceivable a concept as old age: as hard to imagine as an iPhone screen without any messages. They are not alone.

Never mind dying: to me, being old can seem an equally long way off.

Okay, so I'm not the man I once was. I'm a lot stiffer in the limbs; I've fallen out of love with barbecues; and I often mean to say one thing and something completely different comes out of my mouth – a complaint shared by the classical scholar and Professor of Greek at Oxford, Gilbert Murray, who once wrote, 'It is a great nuisance getting old and never knowing whether you haven't said Jerusalem when you meant Paddington.'

I am also only too aware of the many friends I have lost in recent years, and find I have an increasing tendency to pick up on the sort of statistics on health and ageing that get bandied around in the press.

I heard only this morning on the *Today* programme that one in six people suffer strokes. However, I am assured by my doctor that if I take a small dose of statin every day the chances of my having a stroke in the next ten years are considerably reduced. How reassuring is that?

The great humorist Oliver Pritchett wrote wisely – and wittily – on the subject of ageing in his *Sunday Telegraph* column. He had read somewhere that old people feel more fulfilled than ever, that one's sixties are the happiest days of one's life, and that seventy-four is the new thirty-two, and is as sceptical about surveys of this kind as I am.

Having undertaken one of his own (entirely impromptu, as he was the first to admit), he realised that since 68 per cent of people over the age of seventy are usually wearing the wrong glasses when they fill in the forms, for all they know they may be ticking the box that says they have sex three times a week when what they are really trying to say is that they are happy with their dustbin collection.

It's one thing to convince oneself that, at the age of seventy-eight, one is enjoying late middle age, but when will one know when the time has come to give in and admit that one is old?

There have been plenty of wisecracks, along the lines of Bob Hope's 'You know you're getting old when the candles cost more than the cake' variety. In fact, I'd bet that more jokes have been made about old age than about sex, farting and mothers-in-law put together.

And, of course, no discussion on the subject would be complete without Bette Davis's 'Old age ain't no place for sissies,' which I have included only to show how even the most distinguished Americans are not at their best with English grammar.

Whatever any wit has to say on the subject and however good or bad the jokes, old age is not necessarily for old people. It's purely for people who suffer from old age.

I had always imagined that it steals up on you, like a thunderstorm: that you can see it coming from a distance, thereby giving you time to put a few plans into action.

David Niven was of the same persuasion. 'Old age has got to start creeping up on me one day soon,' he said, 'and frankly I'm scared. I don't want to be old. I've always felt so young and I want to stay that way.'

In his case, though, it didn't creep: it struck, in the shape of motor neurone disease, poor chap, thereby adding weight to the general consensus among gerontologists that old age comes on one suddenly, like a malevolent, spiteful and implacable assassin.

In Paolo Sorrentino's film *Youth*, the elderly composer Fred Ballinger, played by Michael Caine, sums it up in less than a dozen words: 'I've become old and I don't know how I got here.'

'It is,' said James Thurber, 'one of the most unexpected of all the things that can happen to a man.'

That being so, and I have no evidence to suppose otherwise, you will appreciate why I was convinced one day last week that the fickle finger of fate had pointed at me as unequivocally and cruelly as Lord Sugar's in his television boardroom.

The evidence was overwhelming. My back was so stiff I could hardly stand upright, let alone do up a shoelace; I had stabbing pains in my left upper thigh; I had suddenly developed a toothache of the kind that in ancient Egypt had strong men calling for a freshly slaughtered mouse to be applied to the offending area; I had one of the most persistent coughs ever; I had a painful crack in my right heel; an ocean-going headache; the tooth next to the aching one (yes, the same one) fell out into a mushroom omelette; oh, and I couldn't remember the word 'plagiarism'.

If that doesn't suggest I should consider revising my bold claims in Chapter One, I don't know what does.

Correction: did. False alarm. A shot across the bows, possibly, but nothing more. Less than a week later I am feeling, if not like a mountain goat on the first day of spring, then certainly like a reasonably contented sheep.

'You're only as old as you look' was one of many platitudes

one used to hear trotted out, and is by far the most nonsensical. While it may be true that some people can retain their younger looks longer than others, a nasty illness or plain genetic make-up or even heavy smoking can make a fifty-year-old look thirty years older.

These days a nip here and a tuck there can remove a few lines and blemishes. (Though as Julian Barnes remarked in a radio talk on the subject of time, 'There's nothing more ageing than a facelift.')

But back in the fifties and sixties people did look exactly what they were – mostly getting on a bit, to say the least.

George Orwell could well have had any number of fellow writers in mind when he declared, 'At fifty, everyone has the face he deserves.' Or as a wise old bird I knew used to say, 'You don't get a face like that for nothing.'

There's no question that older members of one's families all seemed to grow older much more quickly and more obviously than we do nowadays. Everyone did.

From 1946 to 1967, there was a popular radio show called *Have a Go*, in which the actor Wilfred Pickles would interview members of the public, ask them some simple questions and, if they answered them correctly, hand them a small cash prize. Or, rather, he would say, 'Give her [or him] the money, Barney,' and the producer, whose name was Barney Colehan, would hand over a few small notes. He would also give £1. 19s. 11d to anyone prepared to 'share their intimate secrets'. This included their age. Anyone over sixty automatically earned a warm round of applause.

The real reward for sexagenarians, though, was the pleasing prospect of a life of easeful pleasure.

The afternoons in our house when I was in my teens and twenties were quiet times – upstairs as well as down. While my father was in the garden, or in his favourite armchair in front of the TV, my mother would be upstairs on her bed enjoying yet another detective novel and dozing until it was time to come down and get the teapot and the cake out.

That was what I understood by the words 'old age' and still do.

You Silly Old Git

If there's one thing I have discovered about getting older and didn't anticipate to quite the extent I had imagined, it is that there is no way silver hairs are going to earn any respect from the young whatsoever.

To them you are an old fool. You don't know anything. You don't say anything worth listening to. Your jokes are incomprehensible. Your references are meaningless. Your attempts to maintain old-fashioned standards in a world where most people disregard conventions and put two fingers up to rules are at best risible, and at worst contemptible. You are yesterday's man – or woman.

And if, by any chance, you were once somebody, your chances of being given the respect you are due are as slim as anyone else's of your age.

Mind you, the word 'respect' doesn't mean quite the same to today's urban youth as it does to silly old gits like me.

An internet dictionary defines it as 'A feeling of deep admiration for someone or something elicited by their abilities, qualities or achievements.'

Synonyms include 'esteem', 'regard', 'deference' and 'estimation'.

Just so. Here's an example that I feel sure anybody of my age, or near it, would understand without question.

I was once in a post office in Lower Regent Street, long since gone (I mean the post office). It was pretty crowded and customers were having difficulty fighting their way in and out. The situation was not helped by a large population of young people wearing rucksacks.

One elderly man was having a particularly difficult time of it. He was handsome, with short grizzled hair and matching moustache, and wearing a dark overcoat. Having almost been knocked off his feet by a swinging rucksack, he recovered his posture and toddled bravely on into the swirling crowd.

I recognised him at once and would have gone to his aid, had I not felt sure he was not the kind of man to take kindly to special treatment.

'That,' I said to a thirtyish-looking fellow standing in front of me in the so-called queue, 'is possibly one of the most distinguished men you are ever likely to stand next to.'

'Oh yes,' he said, without any obvious interest. 'Who would he be, then, when he's at home?'

'*He*,' I said, 'is the man once known to everyone as plain Alex.'

'Alex who?'

'Earl Alexander of Tunis.'

'Should I have heard of him?'

I said, 'Field Marshal Earl Alexander of Tunis was one of the greatest military commanders of the Second World War. C-in-C Middle East. Supreme Allied Commander

Mediterranean. Governor-General of Canada. Minister of Defence. Governor of the Tower of London.'

'Bloody hell,' said the young man. 'I'm surprised he's allowed out on his own.' By which, presumably, he meant, why isn't he surrounded by a posse of heavies, if not a military escort in full fig?

He was clearly someone whose idea of abilities, qualities and achievements was as far removed from mine as courtly love is from Donald Trump.

The online Urban Dictionary is more in tune with the modern mindset, if the following examples of how to use the word 'respect' are anything to go by:

a) 'I ain't no bitch. How 'bout some motherfucking respect.'

b) Person 1: 'I was banging dumb bitches last night.'
Person 2: 'Respect!'

At least the Urban Dictionary has the grace to give 'top definition' to the word as 'A quality seriously lacking in today's society.'

Time was when respect was something the younger generation instinctively showed to their elders, regardless of their achievements. That's because it was generally held that one's elders were automatically one's betters. And they didn't have to bang drums, dumb bitches or anything else to prove it.

I once stunned my grandson into a state of open-mouthed incredulity when I told him that when I was growing up, a boy or a young man, when introduced to an older man, would invariably address him as 'sir'.

Ludo said, 'The only people I call "sir" are the masters at school.'

I said so did we, and that was why it came naturally to us to call anyone who was older than us 'sir'. I added that if he were at boarding school he would probably find himself calling his mother 'sir' out of pure habit. Or 'matron'.

Indeed, before Mrs Matthew and I were married, and for many years afterwards, I called my father-in-law 'sir'. Had he invited me to call him by his Christian name, I would probably have done so, though not easily. It would not have felt right, somehow. Not that it was up for discussion.

When John Betjeman, having married in secret in 1933, asked his father-in-law how he should address him, the issue was sorted out straight away and in no uncertain terms. But then, men of the calibre of Field Marshal Sir Philip Chetwode, Commander-in-Chief of the army in India, did not get where they were without knowing how to sort out matters of etiquette.

'You can't call me Philip,' he told the young man. 'That would never do. And you can't call me Father, because I'm not your father.' He paused. 'You'd better call me Field Marshal.'

Mind you, he wasn't best pleased that Betjeman had married his daughter anyway. Indeed, he never quite managed to get his son-in-law's name right. Once, when his butler addressed his daughter as 'Miss Penelope', he barked, 'She's not Miss Penelope. She's Mrs Bargeman.'

More than twenty years later, he was still having difficulty with his name. He once offered Betjeman a lift up to town in his car. 'Drop me at the House of Lords,' he told his driver, 'and take Mr Thingummy here where he wants to go.'

Time was when informality from a stranger was a cause for suspicion and discomfort. It was known as 'being familiar'. Even if no disrespect was intended.

When my mother was in her seventies, she came to London to have one of her hips replaced. What is now the Chelsea and Westminster Hospital was in those days St Stephen's, a much smaller and more modest place where a school friend of mine happened to be the head the orthopaedic department.

He did a great job, as I knew he would, and my mother recuperated quickly and easily in the small National Health ward where she was in the warm and gentle hands of kind nurses, many of whom were West Indian.

Living in darkest Norfolk, she didn't see many black people. In fact, I would go so far as to say she had never seen one in real life. So, encountering them daily at close quarters was for her an odd, not to say slightly surreal, experience.

But, of course, once she got to know her nurses she became very fond of them. Never once did she object to being washed and manhandled and seen in embarrassing states of undress, but there was one thing that she could never get used to, and that was their easy use of her Christian name.

'Morning, Doris. How are you feeling, darling?'

Never in all her years had she been addressed with such familiarity by anyone other than close friends and older members of her family, and certainly not by anyone to whom she had not been formally introduced.

I have to confess that, despite having lived through the casual sixties and the careless years that followed, I am at an age when I sympathise with her. I am only too happy to be called Christopher by small children (if it makes them feel more at ease), by their parents, or by fellow dinner-party guests, even if I am meeting them for the first time. Indeed, I cannot think of a single dinner party I have been to in the past forty years when I have not kissed every female guest on departure, regardless of age or distinction, as enthusiastically as if I had known them all my life.

On the other hand, anyone who takes it on him or herself to address me as 'Christopher' – or, even worse, as 'Chris' – when I do not know him or her from Adam is another matter. Perhaps people who do this kind of thing think they are being friendly; if so, they are sadly mistaken.

Actually, I am quite relaxed at being called 'Christopher' by builders. As a horny-handed son of toil myself, I feel very much one of them, and given the amount of time they spend in one's property, and the number of teas, coffees and biscuits we share on an average day, and the fact that I nearly always address them as 'George' or 'Jack' or whatever, I see no reason why, as mates, they shouldn't do the same.

I have only come up against one problem in a long career of builder/buildee relationships and that was some years ago, when a couple of blokes were working on a portico outside the front door of the house we lived in at the time. Rather than waste money on a parking meter for a moment longer than was absolutely necessary, they would park outside the house, with their windows down, drinking tea and reading the *Sun* or the *Mirror* or some such until 8.29, when they would fire up their van and head for the nearest available space.

At some point during their temporary stay I would pass

them on the way to the newsagent's to buy my morning paper, greeting them with a cheery wave, at which the one nearest the pavement would invariably call out 'Morning, Maffews'.

The first time it happened I thought nothing of it. But when it became a daily habit, I found myself thinking I should do something about it. But what?

'Actually, it's Matthew without an *s*,' though true, wouldn't necessarily cut it, as he might then start saying 'Morning Maffew' and we'd be no nearer a satisfactory solution.

'Excuse me, if you don't mind my saying so, it's either "Mr Matthew" or "sir",' though obviously a bit on the heavy-handed side, would have the advantage of making matters clear. It might also have had the disadvantage of the pair of them shoving off and never coming back. Or, worse, making a deliberate mistake and having to come back another time to put it right.

In the end, of course, I did the sensible thing that any right-thinking householder would have done. I smiled, replied 'Good morning' and headed for the newsagent's.

The Boycott Effect

Anyone who has ever spent more than ten minutes listening to *TMS* (*Test Match Special* for the uninitiated) while Geoffrey Boycott, the legendary Yorkshire opening batsman, is in full flow will know what I mean by the phrase the Boycott Effect.

It invariably begins with the words 'In my day ...' and leads into a long and detailed critique of a batsman's shot that has just got him out, followed by an account of how differently he would have played it in his day and how his mum could have played it better with a stick of rhubarb.

'I'm not blaming the lad,' he'll continue, 'but ...' and on he will go to blame the lad and relive the golden days in the sixties when he was opening the batting for England and helmets hadn't been invented and if you got hit on the head by a ball travelling at 90 mph, you just gave it a rub and got on with it. ('My mum got hit on the head five times a day every day of her life and she never once complained, or wore a helmet.')

You didn't call for the physio to come out and waste everyone's time with painkillers and soothing sprays, and you certainly didn't leave the field just because you needed to spend a penny. You tied a knot in it and kept going. ('My mum went to the lavatory once when she got up and once when she went to bed and she lived to be a hundred.')

Men were men in Geoffrey's day and they behaved like men. 'If you were given out when I was playing for Yorkshire and England, you were out. You didn't go appealing straight away and standing around waiting for the television match official to go through his tedious routine because you thought the umpire needed his eyes testing. You walked.'

Oh, and just because it was 93 degrees out in the middle in Chennai ('or Madras, as I still like to call it') and as humid as a baby's nappy, you didn't need to stop and have a drink every two minutes and change your gloves and rub your face with a towel. You were playing a Test match against the Indians, not dancing the Gay Gordons at a deb dance in the Dorchester.

'Hot and tired? My arse. The only time my mum was hot and tired was when she fell asleep in the bath listening to *Mrs Dale's Diary.*'

Someone once warned me many years ago, in the days when the idea of being old was, to me, unimaginable, that when launching into a reminiscence about one's youth, two phrases that should never cross one's lips are 'In my day, of course . . . ' or 'When I was your age . . . ' (and, if you happen to be a retired Test cricketer, 'When I was playing for England . . . '). Indeed, anything that might suggest that everything was better when we were lads is to be avoided.

I am proud to say that I have never once lapsed unwittingly into reminiscence with the young and I intend to keep it that way. On the other hand, if someone asks me a direct question about some aspect of my past life, I feel it would be churlish to say 'I'm sorry, I don't talk about the past. It's a foreign country. They do things differently there, etc.' Churlish, pompous and uncalled for. It is the duty of a grandfather to reminisce from time to time.

So, when Tug informed me that she had to write an essay about what is was like to be brought up in the war, I could hardly refuse.

'Of course,' I said. 'When you say "war", do you mean the Second World War?'

'Grandpa,' she said, in a tone of the sort teenage girls use when addressing a dim younger sibling, 'were you a child in any other war?'

Having for a short time taught Latin and Scottish dancing in a prep school in the Home Counties back in the late fifties, I became used to being put on the back foot by the young.

What a schoolboy enjoys more than anything is making a perfectly intelligent and kind-hearted, if slightly naïve, member of staff look a complete arse.

I remember an eleven-year-old by the name of Feltwell asking me in all seriousness if I knew why cats always stuck their tails up in the air when you stroked them. Naturally I assumed this to be a zoological matter – something to do with the sex lives of cats, perhaps; or maybe it was a reaction to being touched on a particular part of its anatomy.

Feltwell was a clever boy, inclined to dig somewhat deeper into some subjects than others in B1, so having been on the arts side of school myself, and knowing next to nothing about zoology, or indeed science of any kind, I took his question seriously, imagining that he would tell me something inter-esting, if not useful.

'No, I don't know, actually, Feltwell,' I said. 'Why does a cat stick its tail up in the air when you stroke its back?'

'Well, sir,' said Feltwell, 'if it didn't, your hand would fall off the end.'

It's all very well for these clever-clogs boys to make their elders and betters look foolish in the eyes of their fellow members of staff, but try riposting and you find yourself accused of mental cruelty, if not worse.

Another brainy boy in the scholarship form asked in the middle of lunch if I knew what circumcision was. In the middle of lunch!

I'd been caught out by him on more than one occasion, so I lobbed the question straight back into his court.

'David,' I said, with a faint sigh, 'you obviously know what it is, so why are you asking me?'

'Well, sir, I looked it up in the *Encyclopaedia Britannica* and it said "*Removal of the foreskin according an ancient Jewish custom.*"'

This produced, as I daresay he had intended all along, general hilarity along the length of our table. I'm glad to say I kept my cool.

'So you *do* know what it is,' I said. 'What else do you want to know?'

He squinted through his wonky National Health specs at Miss May – an elderly woman with a bun and a bust who was responsible for teaching some of the eight- and nine-year-olds – who was sitting at the end of a nearby table.

'Well, sir,' he said, 'do you suppose Miss May has had her foreskin removed according to an ancient Jewish custom?'

By this stage I was getting rather bored with the subject,

and the giggling, and the lunch, so I decided to fob him off with a dismissive remark to which there could be no comeback.

'I've no idea, David,' I said distractedly. 'Why don't you ask her yourself?'

Well, how did I know the idiot was going to take me literally? Miss May ignored me for the rest of term in a manner that I can only describe as pointed.

The thought vaguely crossed my mind that teenaged Tug might be amused to know what it was like for an eighteen-year-old straight out of school to be hired as a junior master in a country prep school in the late fifties. More fun than the war, surely?

I put it to her.

'Maybe,' she said. 'I'll ask Ludo. LUDO!'

There was a longish silence on the line, then,

'Are you still there, Grandpa?'

I said I was.

'Ludo says that thinking about school at the weekend might be rather boring. He'd rather hear about the war.'

'The war's over,' I said. 'For today, anyway.'

Body Language

I was idly peeling a tangerine the other day when I had a thought of a magnitude that might have struck Einstein in one of his better moments. The peel itself was soft, loose and flabby. The fruit inside was more or less unattached, and, more to the point, I pretty well knew before a single segment had come near my teeth that it was beyond its use-by date: dried up, tasteless and unattractive.

The first bite confirmed my fears. And my theory.

Old bodies are like old tangerines: acceptable when clothed; once in the birthday suit, thoroughly unappetising.

It's never anyone's fault: it's all down to gravity. However many hours one spends in the gym, no matter how many calories one denies oneself, and elderflowers one chooses instead of pints, and miles one jogs, science calls the shots.

I had a friend, of about my age, who decided he was carrying a dangerous amount of weight and put himself on the mother and father of all diets. All I can surmise is that most of it must have been on his face and neck because the next time I saw him he was almost unrecognisable: drawn, haggard, hollow-cheeked, almost cadaverous. The opportunity to inspect his limbs and torso was not available, but I'd bet good money that his skin was hanging down in folds like a half-open blind.

On the plus side, his clothes had never looked better on him. Nor did his ferocious diet, which he insisted on maintaining, have any obvious effect on his demeanour, which has remained as benign as ever.

Still, it makes me wonder whether any man beyond a certain age should worry about his looks. Or rather it did until I walked into the changing room at a golf club one day to find it populated almost entirely by naked men, all of them well over sixty.

Friends who I had always thought of as being well proportioned, if not actually slim, had suddenly developed enormous stomachs and pendulous breasts. The thinner ones looked like white candles that had been left alight for too long; beefier types who I had imagined (not that I spend much time imagining what people of my age look like without their clothes on) to be well muscled and wouldn't look amiss in the ring during a top-flight World Wrestling Entertainment match were so well endowed with belly fat that one wondered how they'd manage to swing a cat, let alone a five iron.

More startling than the sight of all this unfamiliar and unseemly flesh was the fact than none of its owners showed the slightest sign of bashfulness. They would not have looked out of place in a painting by Lucian Freud.

(I have no hard evidence one way or the other, but I am assured that women in similar situations can often behave just as brazenly.)

Am I alone in thinking that if I find my own body unattractive, then to parade it in front of others is at best uncivil and at worst offensive?

Were I blessed with a torso that looked as if I had made a serious effort to tone it, I might go so far as to take my shirt off in front of my peers – but only before putting on another one.

And if, for some unknown reason, I were to decide to take a shower after a round of golf, it surely wouldn't require too much effort to tuck a towel round my waist.

On the subject of body toning, am I already too old to join a gym or hire a personal trainer? No one who knows me well could accuse me of narcissism, but I had a bit of a shock recently when I snapped up a pair of blue corduroy trousers (36 inch waist, 31 leg) reduced by a handsome twenty pounds in a sale, only to find that I couldn't do them up. I had always understood that after a certain age you retain roughly the same waist size. Clearly mistakenly. The twenty pounds I had saved went immediately on the two inches I had to have added to the waistband.

Dieting is a bore at any age, and doubly so when you're in your seventies, but a regular visit to a gym would offer a fresh and interesting challenge, new friendships and a 36-inch waist, or even less.

By coincidence there was a long article in the *Times* magazine last year entitled 'Abs fab: the year men became obsessed with their bodies'.

The cover of the magazine featured four muscly and purposeful-looking young men posing in variously coloured knee-length trunks. It seems they were first seen in a poster in London Underground stations, advertising a men's fitness company which, if you were to take advantage of their services, would transform you into lean, ripped specimens like them.

The campaign apparently aroused considerable resentment among thirty-something blokes confronted daily by these magnificent examples of manhood, who felt that these four, far from inspiring them to do something about their own white, desk-bound, flabby torsos, were in fact 'bodyshaming' them.

Speaking for myself, it would be hard to imagine anyone more ashamed of his body that yours truly. It wasn't helped by the tactless headmaster of my prep school who, during a gym lesson, uttered the unforgettable (to me) words, 'Come on, pull your shoulders back. Not you, Matthew. You don't have any.'

In those days, body-building was beyond the wildest imagination of twelve-year-olds. The only person anyone had ever heard of who had done it and encouraged others to follow his example was a man called Charles Atlas, who, if his publicity was to be believed, had once been a 97-pound weakling, and was once sitting on a beach with a young woman when a beefy guy walked by and kicked sand in his face. So humiliated was he by this experience that he determined it was never going to happen again, and to this end he built himself into a man mountain.

Whether he ever encountered his tormentor again is not recorded. However, he attracted a lot of followers – though I was not one of them.

Indeed, among my friends, body-building was merely a source for jokes.

Looking back, I rather wish I had given it a try, though reading the *Times* article, it would seem that beefing oneself up is not the ideal solution for low self-esteem. A lot of large, muscular men apparently suffer agonising self-consciousness in the belief that they are small, if not weedy. This condition is known in the body-building business as 'bigorexia'.

I would suggest that people of my age suffer from a similar condition: gerontorexia.

At the time of writing, this word does not, as far as I am aware, appear in any dictionary, medical or otherwise, and I am rather hoping that whoever is appointed to edit the next supplement of the *Oxford English Dictionary* will consider it as an entry to describe a sense of hopelessness experienced by the over-seventies when they realise that they are never going to be beach fit; they will never know the joys of the bench press; they have better things to do with the ever-dwindling years than fuss about delts, abs, lats and biceps and throw good money after bad as a gym bunny at some expensive health centre or other; and that they should settle for what they've got and be thankful they are still on their feet.

Decline and Sprawl

Having taken on this investigation into incipient old age, I thought I should discover – mainly for my own purposes, but also for anybody else in their seventies who happens to be reading this – what old age is. From a purely scientific point of view, that is. If nothing else, it might help me to recognise it when it comes along

I typed the words 'What happens to the body in old age' into Google, and there was the answer. Or rather, answers. According to the Science Museum, no less. Should there be any lingering doubt about the state of one's decrepitude, here is an obvious one to be getting on with:

> Because your skin gets thinner and less elastic, it gets wrinkly and drier because it makes less oil and sweat. And because you store less fat under your skin, your bones become more visible. These, like your muscles, get weaker and your immune system can't fight disease as well as it used to. Also, your features change.

You'll notice the use of the words 'you' and 'your'. There is nothing personal in this. Some scientists favour the second person plural to refer to old people in general. Personally, when talking about the human body, I would say 'we' and 'our', though frankly I am not entirely convinced that much of the above is relevant to me. Were I to look into a mirror to find I am the spitting image of W. H. Auden, I would be the first to agree that my skin is thinner and less elastic than of old. I can see no sign of being any bonier.

I suppose my features have changed slightly over the years. When I was a small boy, for instance, both my ears stuck out like a pair of taxi doors (to quote the famous Bing Crosby analogy). But then you only have to look at one of my prep-school photographs – of, say, 1949, as Ludo and I were doing one day – and the first thing that will strike you is that virtually all the boys had sticky-out ears.

'And very short hair,' said Ludo. 'Was that because of nits?'

I said that we didn't have nits in those days. Not in the better parts of Surrey, anyway. But we did have very bad hairdressing. It was no use asking to have your hair cut in a particular way. Everyone had a short back and sides, whether they liked it or not. The school barber would arrive and spend the entire day cropping boys' heads with the speed of an Australian sheep-shearing champion.

Ludo said, 'Some of my friends have a short back and sides but their ears don't stick out like that.'

I explained that, in those days, schoolmasters were entitled to dish out minor forms of punishment as and when they thought fit, and suggested that the reason everyone's ears stuck out as much as they did was a direct result of our headmaster's fondness for grabbing any lughole that happened to be within arm's length and giving it a sharp and extremely painful tweak. In fact, it was often more a pull or a wrench than a tweak.

Having brought tears to the victim's eyes and an involuntary 'Ow, sir!', the headmaster would give his fingers a look of total disgust, as if he had just come into contact with dog mess. His face would have an expression of furious repulsion as he muttered 'Uuurgh!' and shook his hand, as though to rid himself of every last trace of this revolting foreign body.

'Perhaps that's because some boys did have nits,' Ludo persisted. 'Everyone gets them now, so I don't see why they shouldn't have got them when you were at school.'

There are times when there's no arguing with the young.

I don't know if any of those boys suffered from protruding-ear syndrome in later life. One did hear of people having to have minor operations to pin their ears back. Mine seemed to flatten themselves of their own accord – unless of course it was the result of my head growing to accommodate them. Otherwise, it seems to me that my features have changed very little over the years.

There are those whose looks in old age have changed out of all recognition. This is particularly so if they lose their hair; or grow beards, of course – something that has tempted me only once, many years ago, when I thought it might be interesting to see what I looked like with a full beaver. A local in our village in Suffolk saw me one day when I was still at the heavily unshaven stage and greeted me with 'Christ, you look terrible.'

Beards apart, the most obvious cause of facial transformation is fat: not just over the cheeks and under the eyes and round the jaw, but under it as well. This manifests itself in a variety of styles that speak for themselves. Plucked at random from the 1245 listed synonyms in the Urban Dictionary, here are a few of the less offensive versions of the double chin and turkey neck: the fat scarf, the meat beard, the throtum, the fatkerchief, the double whopper. There's also the neckfurter, but that is usually reserved for the roll at the back of the neck, especially when it is sweaty and particularly frankfurter-like in appearance.

Older women enjoy their own lexicon of euphemisms, not least to describe the flaps of skin that hang under the triceps, such as bingo wings, tuck-shop arms and arm charms.

These are not necessarily confined to the elderly (or to women, in the case of bingo wings, which I seem to be developing despite never having played bingo in my life, or indeed been a woman), but ageing is a major factor.

I feel convinced that, fundamentally, my face has changed little over the years. I've got a few lines round the mouth and eye area – mainly caused by laughter, I'm glad to say – and I'd like to think that people have no difficulty remembering me when I meet them after a long separation. Obviously I have to jog their memories sometimes by actually revealing my name, but not always by any means.

As for my own memory, well, which of us can honestly say that we could remember the name of the wife of Richard I without a helpful clue? (Answer: Berengaria of Navarre, of course. Daughter of Sancho VI. But then you probably knew that already.)

The list of symptoms doesn't end there. If we are to believe the brainbox at the Science Museum who put it together, our feet get longer and wider as we get older; our ears stretch down and the tips of our noses lengthen and droop; we sneeze more; we clear our throats more; we grow senile warts that look like moles; our teeth get longer; men's voices get higher and women's voices get lower; and we get watery eyes. This is due to the age-related narrowing of our tear ducts – though I'd wager that in many cases it's people weeping for their lost youth.

Oh, I almost forgot: good news – the older we become, the quicker we get drunk.

Far be it from me – a scientific ignoramus – to take issue with anybody as distinguished as the Science Museum, but if my seventy-eight-year-old chassis is anything to go by, there are a number of symptoms that they seem to have failed to take into account. To wit: thickening toenails; night cramp which comes from nowhere, seems to have no obvious cause and can be more agonising that being shot in the leg (not that I have ever been shot anywhere, but I can't think of anything more painful to compare it with); cataracts, which seem to affect everyone over seventy; and veins.

I appear to have been gifted with a larger selection of veins than most: I couldn't have been more colourfully tattooed by Dame Nature. Luckily for me, none of them seem to be varicose, just ornamental. Indeed, drying my left leg after a shower the other day, I noticed to my astonishment that some tiny veins on the inside of my left foot had formed themselves into letters of the alphabet: a definite C, a very creditable M ... Could I be the first man ever to have a monogrammed circulatory system?

Of all the words of wisdom attributed on the Science Museum's site to the brightest scientific brains in the country, the one that rings the loudest bell for me is what they tactfully refer to as 'being disturbed in the night', which in layman's terms means getting up at three in the morning for a widdle.

This is a subject which I had been hoping would not have to be raised among my peers, but since they are nearly all suffering from the same problem – men *and* women – I am probably on fairly safe ground.

I had always assumed that there were two simple reasons for this annoying encumbrance: one, that it was to do with one's prostate, and/or two, sufferers simply had weak bladders. But now I discover that it is simply another sign of the ageing process: as we get older our kidneys produce too much urine at night.

This is all very reassuring, but, as explanations go, it doesn't go any way towards helping us get a good night's sleep – something which I look back on as fondly as I look back on my first duffel coat.

It always used to be said that the older one gets, the less sleep one needs.

If this is true, then I have nothing to worry about. Or do I? It seems that older adults require the same amount of sleep as young adults – between seven and nine hours, which tallies with the perceived wisdom that eight hours of sleep at night is what we should be aiming for. In fact, the average person gets six and half hours, and many manage on five or six. Mrs Thatcher needed a mere four. Perhaps she never felt the need to get up in the night for any reason, and being asleep for only four, why would she have done?

Being the creature of clear-mindedness and positive thinking that she was, I presume she didn't lie awake wondering if anyone was ever to find Mark in the Sahara, or if Carol was happy with her latest boyfriend, or what to do about Geoffrey Howe. Some of us, however, are born worriers, and the tiniest problems can have me staring into the dark. The other night I was awake for a full hour, arguing with myself about whether I was going deaf or having an ear wax problem.

Actually, I wasn't worrying about that *all* the time, but that's how it started before leading to a worry about my health in general, whether the knocking noise in the car was anything serious, and had one left it too late at seventy-eight to be tackling Proust for the first time?

There is another commonly held belief that if you fall asleep in front of the *Antiques Roadshow*, or have forty winks at tea-time, you won't sleep properly at night. I can find no clinical response one way or another to this old chestnut (if indeed that is what it is), and I shall continue to believe that a zizz after lunch, sprawled in a large armchair, is the one of greatest pleasures known to man.

Postscript: Typically, Ludo wanted to know if it is possible to postpone old age. The general consensus would be no, but who knows what science might come up with in future years? The growth hormones that control bone growth and protein production pack up any time between sixty and ninety. Women can take HRT to relieve the effects of the menopause, and one day growth hormones might be used to slow the ageing process, and then future generations can look forward to sitting in a chair, deaf and half blind, wondering why they bothered.

Compared with our Stone Age ancestors, whose lives were extremely dangerous and extremely short, we all live to a great enough age already. The average life span is over seventy-seven for men and eighty-two for women, though a hundred people have lived for at least 114 years.

The record for the world's oldest human being was once held by a French woman called Jeanne Calment, who lived in Arles and died in August 1997 at the age of 122 years and 164 days and, who knows, could have passed a fully eared Van Gogh in the street without so much as a second glance.

An Italian woman by the name of Emma Morano looked set at one time to challenge Madame Calment for the title, but died in April 2017 at a mere 117 years and 137 days. She started working at the age of thirteen, spinning jute for potato sacks, until the damp atmosphere made her ill and she was told by a doctor that she would not live long.

Women, it would seem, have always outlived men and for a long time it was believed that no man had ever lived beyond 116, until an ancient resident of Central Java by the name of Mbah Gotho died shortly after Signora Morano at the astonishing age of 146.

He outlived his four wives, ten siblings and five children, and was a heavy smoker to the very end.

Grumpy Old Man

'Hello, Grandpa.'

It's the sort of voice that one always hopes to hear on the other end of the telephone line, but rarely does.

'How are you?'

Others enquire politely; none are so obviously keen to know the answer as my granddaughter.

'I'm very well. How are you?'

'I'm good.'

They all say that now. The young do, anyway. It's another of those expressions that everyone uses without thinking. No point in saying anything, though. You only end up sounding like a retired schoolmaster. Which, I suppose, in a way I am.

'Literally' is another word that gets chucked around without any thought as to its meaning, as in 'I was literally having kittens'. And don't get me started on 'beg the question'. No one seems to care that it is *not* another way of saying 'raise the question'.

I recently tried to explain to one of my thirty-something sons that 'begging the question', or *petitio principii*, is a fallacy committed when an arguer includes the conclusion to be proven within a premise of the argument, often in an indirect way, such that its presence within the premise is hidden or at least not easily apparent. To put it more simply, when someone attempts to prove a proposition on a premise that itself requires proof. Often referred to as *hysteron proteron*.

An obvious example, I suggested, might be, 'Opium induces sleep because it has a soporific quality.'

'Right,' he said, in a tone that clearly suggested 'why waste money on opium when you're around?'

Small wonder that I have so far avoided commenting on the careless use of 'disinterested' when someone really means 'uninterested'. I can put up with 'prestigious' being used to mean 'distinguished' even though it really means 'deceptive' (from prestidigitation, or conjuring). But just because it sounds like the French word *jeune*, jejune does not mean 'young'. It means 'scanty' or 'meagre'.

The thing that drives me more potty than anything is the constant mispronunciation of 'contribute' and 'distribute'? For heaven's sake: the emphasis is – or should be – on the second syllable. The emphasis is on the first syllable only when you use the noun – contribution, distribution.

Almost everyone manages to get it wrong these days, not least so-called professional broadcasters. Whatever happened to the BBC's pronunciation unit? Never mind the ongoing debate about whether or not foreigners coming to live in this country should be able to speak English: a lot of the English aren't much good at it either. The standards are dropping daily.

And while I'm on the subject of standards, I can't resist

a few words on the way men, who are old enough to know better, dress these days.

In 1983 I wrote a book entitled *How to Survive Middle Age*, in the course of which I identified a certain type of man who I described as an LCT. It stands for last-chance trendy – a type who will go to inordinate lengths to try to persuade the rest of the world that he is still as much in the swim of things as ever; or, if he never was, then he would like to be before it's too late.

I said that he was all too easy to spot and picked out a few of his ill-advised attempts to keep up with the younger generation: the figure-hugging shirts, unbuttoned to the breastbone, the better to display the gold bullion nestling among the greying chest hairs; the denim jacket; the Indian silk scarf gathered at the throat; the hand-tooled belt over which the paunch oozes like baker's dough from a bread tin; the hair trained up and over the head in an unconvincing attempt to disguise the bald pate; the Zapata moustache . . .

In those days I was describing a forty-five-year-old who couldn't bear to think he was no longer twenty years younger.

I may well have succumbed to some of those feelings myself, and to those terrible outfits (though in my defence, I never went as far as a moustache, and I think I have already made the point about my hair in no uncertain terms). But as we middle-agers grew older and greyer and more self-conscious, we put away childish thoughts of reversing time. And now that we're getting older . . .

Well, we don't sport medallions, or silk scarves, or Zapata moustaches, but we do dress a lot differently from the way our own parents did. Women just as much as men, if not more so.

Time was, and not so long ago as all that, when a woman

reached seventy she, like many others of her age, changed into a costume that was almost as strict as a nun's habit: long black or grey garments that made it clear to one and all that she was no longer attractive.

Men would get up every day and slip into their own old-age ensemble. It consisted of corduroy trousers (brown or beige), a discreetly coloured and heavily darned pullover, checked shirt, tie or cravat, brown or suede brogues and, if they were going out anywhere, a sports jacket (often with patches on the elbows). There were obviously variations on a theme, but not many. The point was, you could recognise a retired or elderly type from a mile away.

These days they are as likely to dress in the same style as their children, if not their grandchildren. Jeans, shirts hanging outside their trousers, T-shirts (sometimes alone under a jacket), and brightly coloured gym shoes.

I'm not suggesting that I am totally averse to the odd touch of LCT-ism myself. I have never owned a pair of jeans, and my neck starts itching at the very thought of a jacket over a T-shirt. But I have to admit I have a pair of what are usually classified as trainers – though the only training I do is walking for an hour every day, and because I have got to the age when my feet look and feel about as smooth and supple as Will Kempe's after he'd Morris danced from London to Norwich, the pleasure of a good brisk walk is all the better for a pair of top-quality trainers.

It goes without saying that it would be a creature of poor self-respect who did not wear a suit and tie and polished shoes if he was off to a business meeting, or a formal lunch, or a funeral or whatever; though here again one does see men in suits and open-necked shirts at the most inappropriate occasions. Even with evening wear. Often when sported by show business personalities.

If I receive an invitation with the instruction 'Black tie', I know exactly how I am supposed to dress: a dinner jacket (double-breasted in my case), proper evening-dress trousers, and a black evening bow tie.

I wear this, as I have done all my life, with a button-up dress shirt with a collar, long sleeves and wrist cuffs. (I prefer the pimply variety, but the Venetian blind option is perfectly acceptable.)

For reasons of their own, a lot of people these days favour what I believe is known as a 'wing collar' dress shirt, which isn't anything like a real wing collar of the sort one wears with evening tails, and leaves the tie bands fully visible and, frankly, rather scruffy.

Once, aged about fourteen, I went to stay with a school friend who lent me a clip-on bow tie in a snappy black and white bird's eye design when we went on an outing by Green Line bus to Hampton Court. I felt quite dandyish all day, until it was time to leave. My friend went off to buy something and I was standing near the bus stop when a man came up to me and said, '*Evening Standard* please, mate.'

We all make mistakes when we're young and don't know any better, and I really can't believe that any man of my age would be seen dead in a made-up bow tie, though I wouldn't put it past anyone these days.

Someone recently accused me of being a grumpy old man, no different from Jeremy Clarkson and John Humphrys and Will Self and Arthur Smith in that TV series. Perhaps the older I get, the more I feel like one. And, yes, I am, as Ludo once suggested, rather old-fashioned. But not about everything, I hope.

When in Alan Bennett's *Forty Years On* the headmaster is shocked by the suggestion of sex education in the school play and the housemaster, Franklin, suggests that his standards may perhaps be a little out of date, the headmaster replies, 'Of course they're out of date. Standards always are out of date. That is what makes them standards. I am as broad-minded as the next man, but I have heard matters discussed here which ought never to be mentioned, except in the privacy of one's own bathroom, and even then in hushed tones.'

His school was not, as he is at pains to remind Franklin, Liberty Hall; but modern Britain is not far off.

Oh dear. I'm beginning to sound increasingly like a GOM myself. Only the other day I worked myself up into quite a state when someone who should have known better wrote me a letter, asking me a favour, and managed to spell my surname wrong twice.

I shouldn't really complain. Even in later life, when he was arguably one of the most famous writers in the world, poor old Evelyn Waugh had to put up with people writing about him on the assumption that he was a woman. In one instance, a so-called critic, no less.

Waugh commented in a letter to the *Times Literary Supplement*, in response to the review, 'My Christian name, I know, is occasionally regarded by people of limited social experience as belonging exclusively to one or other sex; but it is unnecessary to go further into my book than the paragraph charitably placed inside for the guidance of un-leisured critics to find my name with the correct prefix of "Mr".'

Squirrels Hiding Nuts in Grass

When boys of Ludo's age consider e-mails to be as out-of-date as Anglo-Saxon, it means that a lot of grandfathers I know are going to have to find different ways of contacting their grandchildren in a hurry. In my case, it's beginning to look as if I might well have to buy an up-to-date, state-of-the-art mobile phone, and learn how to use it.

I had a nasty feeling this was going to happen sooner or later, and that I was no longer going to have to put up with the jaw-dropping looks I get from the young whenever I get my faithful old Nokia 3120 out, and remarks along the lines of 'Oh, is that where you put the coal in?'

I am far from alone. We were recently at a rather smart London party – champagne, lots of famous faces, enough eats so you wouldn't have to worry about supper afterwards – and I was talking to a distinguished fellow humorist friend of mine about this and that when he suddenly stopped and put his hand in his jacket pocket.

'Sorry,' he said. 'I've got my wife's telephone in here and it keeps going off. It could be urgent, but she's on the other side of the room and I can't do anything about it because I don't know how these things work.'

If he had said he didn't know how to tie his shoelaces the reaction from a nearby guest could not have been more incredulous.

'How pretentious can you get?' he squawked.

The humorist protested mildly that he really didn't know how it worked. He didn't have one himself, he had no reason to use one, and he had no plans for doing so in the future.

I fingered my little grey Nokia with its tiny screen and even tinier letters and numbers, which I happened to have brought with me in case of an emergency. I can't imagine what kind of emergency might require a telephone call in the middle of a party: drunkenness and disability, perhaps? A sausage stick in the eye? A heart attack at the sight of Joanna Lumley?

Besides, were anything to happen to me that might necessitate calling an ambulance, pretty well anyone in the room would have an iPhone on them and be able to do it in seconds. Except for me and my humorist friend, that is.

You'll notice I used the term 'mobile phone', because that is what mine is – nothing more, nothing less. I'm told there are some simple games on it, which I have yet to discover for myself, but nothing else. You can't take photographs with it, or receive or send e-mails, or find out what time the next 19 bus is due. It's a telephone, and I use it on the rare occasions I want to telephone somebody or am expecting a call. The latter rarely happens because, nine times out of ten, I have forgotten to turn it on. This is not down to perversity, merely that a) I have never got used to the idea of telephoning people in public, any more than I can get used to the idea of eating in public or walking in the street drinking coffee out of a plastic cup; and b) because I can't think of a single person I want to ring or who wants to ring me. And even if anybody did, the chances are they wouldn't be able to because they don't know my mobile number. Nor do I, which is why I haven't got round to giving it to anyone.

This is as far as I have entered into the magic realm of social networking. I am not on Facebook, nor has anyone ever asked me to be; no one I know is on Instagram or Snapchat or Voodoo or WhatsApp, and I wouldn't have any snippets of information, or photographs, or videos, or questions to send them in the unlikely event of my or their ever being on any of them.

There is another good reason why I don't want to take even the tiniest step in that direction, and that is because I don't wish to become one of those people you see on every bus or Tube, in every pub and café, on every pavement and every room of every house up and down the land, sitting staring blankly at screens, tapping away at tiny keys, while the world goes by unnoticed.

What is this world if, full of care,
We have no time to stand and stare.

Last October was one of the best ever for autumn colours. The trees everywhere were hung with more gold and red and brilliant yellow than I can remember in fifty years of living in London. I walked in Kensington Gardens nearly every day with the dog and who do I see wandering past me? Screen-gogglers and button-tappers. Are they looking about them, breathtaken at nature's seasonal finale? Are they hell. They are checking the sixty-five messages that have arrived between the time they got off the bus or out of the car, crossed the road and entered through the park gates.

What is the matter with everyone these days? Why do they want to know what everyone they know is doing every moment of the day? And not just the people they know: the hundreds of others who are their 'friends', who they will never meet or see and have never heard of. It's all so narcissistic and self-indulgent.

It's not just the teenagers and the young who can't let a nanosecond go by without having another long look: their parents are doing it too.

And, what's more, encouraging their young to start at an increasingly early age.

A friend of mine was travelling on a long train journey recently, sitting next to a young woman and her toddler of about eighteen months. While the woman occupied herself with her screen, her child squawked. Very loudly. All the time.

My friend, a kindly man concerned for the well-being of his fellow man, wondered if perhaps he could help in some way. Pick the child up, perhaps, and bounce it on his knee. Sing it a song. Tell it a story. Devise a simple game.

He was on the point of offering his services when the mother reached into an inside pocket and pulled out another device which she switched on and handed to the child, who in turn started pecking at the screen and tapping the keys and didn't utter another sound for the entire journey.

Presumably there will come a time, not so long from now, when life will be even fuller of care and everyone will still be standing, and sitting, and lounging, and staring at screens signifying nothing.

It could be the death of wonder and imagination. Knowing too much about others, and seeing too much, and hearing too much engenders unnecessary pain and frustration. The girl who has just been given the boot by her boyfriend is sad enough as it is, without seeing pictures posted by her beloved of himself and the girl he has booted her for.

Too much information too easily acquired.

Is that it? Am I done? Not quite. I have one other worry. About e-mails.

They so easy, they're so quick and they're so cheap, everyone writes them.

Well, I say 'writes': pecks them out like a pigeon in Trafalgar Square. Not to read, and keep, and get out at a later date to read again. They are not letters, they are shorthand notes, penned – or rather not penned, that's the whole point – in haste and without love.

What will become of the art of the biographer when everyone has stopped writing real letters – as they surely will – and there aren't even any saved e-mails from or to anyone to draw on? What will become of the art of letter-writing? Are we doomed never to have any more collections of letters by and to the great and the good? *Où sont les épistoliers d'antan*? *Où* indeed.

In my day, of course, (sorry, but it had to come sooner or later) we all wrote letters from an early age. Especially those of us who were sent off to boarding school. Once a week, usually on Sunday mornings, we sat at our desks and wrote to our parents. We were hardly budding Paddy Leigh Fermors, but we were encouraged to be informative and interesting as well as begging – to be sent more sweets, or to be taken away, or whatever the latest need. I don't remember ever speaking to my parents on a telephone.

We also wrote thank-you letters to our grandparents and aunts and uncles and said how pleased we were with their presents and told them what Christmas had been like and wished them a happy new year, and they often replied to say how much our writing had improved. Do today's children still write letters, or do they text Granny and Grandpa? Or, worse, send them an Instagram? And, if they do, do Granny and Grandpa read them – or even get them?

Indeed, will they ever manage to keep up? The latest trend in the gadget world (sorry, Tug and Ludo, but that's how I think of them) is for voice-controlled devices targeted at OAPs. My spies at the annual Consumer Electronics Show in Las Vegas report that it is now possible not only to set your shower at precisely the right temperature by sending a message from your telephone (to your shower, presumably), but you save yourself the trouble of stepping on the pedal of your rubbish bin by simply telling it to open. I am even more thrilled to know that, when the time comes, I shall be able to buy a walking stick that will monitor my every movement and, if a problem arises, will get in touch with my carer; and that in the event of my going a purler, a belt round my waist will inflate so I won't bust my hip. Again.

I am beginning to think it's only a matter of time before today's children are operating their own lives via similar devices. Walking in Hyde Park early one Saturday morning I saw half a dozen would-be horsemen and women from a local riding school. Clearly beginners, they were moving at a pace only slightly nippier than a snail's.

The woman at the front – the instructor, I assumed – had turned in her saddle and was chatting with the rider immediately behind her. The rest were spread out in a kind of equine crocodile. A slightly overweight boy bringing up the rear was slumped in his seat, concentrating on tapping out a message on his iPhone – to his pony, perhaps, telling it when to trot, how to turn left or right, and to let him know if it is planning to do anything silly, like trying to chuck him off onto the sandy surface of Rotten Row.

I'm prepared to believe anything these days.

To the Manners Born

Just down the street from us lives a very rich man. He has an enormous house, an enormous car, and an enormous driver with a very loud voice.

One evening, not long ago, he parked his employer's enormous car in such a way that there was no space left for anyone else. It was a pity, because I was rather hoping to park there myself. He got out of the car and stood looking thoroughly pleased with himself.

'No chance of moving up a bit, I suppose?' I called out.

'Fuck off,' he said.

There seemed little point in arguing the matter further. Not with him, anyway. As I was walking up the street I heard him shouting: 'If you want to talk to me, come here and do it to my face.' I walked on. 'That's right,' he shouted. 'Walk away, why don't you, you fucking old fool?'

Now, I don't know about you, but I think it's quite rude to talk to someone like that. Never mind that I'm a resident, and that my white hair might prompt someone to think I am an old-age pensioner. Indeed, there are often occasions when

I do something really stupid and think what a fool I am. But that's for me to decide.

Still, that's the way it is these days. People do what they want. If a pathway in the local park says, quite clearly, NO CYCLING, and someone wants to cycle down it, they do. Chances are there's no one around to stop them. I don't mean a parks policeman; they're never around. I mean a member of the public. One can try. The best one can hope for is to be told to perform an impossible act on oneself; the worst is to be run over, or punched. Or both.

Indeed, being over seventy is no guarantee one will get off with anything less than a stinging rebuke. If not a stinging ear.

If there's one thing guaranteed to be awarded two fingers more than white hair it's what is now called a posh voice. Nothing rankles more than what used to be known as a public school accent.

When the Leeds Modern School pupil Alan Bennett arrived at Oxford in the late fifties to sit an entrance scholarship exam, he was struck by what he took to be the natural air of superiority of the public school boys – a breed he had heard of but never before encountered. A lot of it could probably be put down to nerves, but to the timid son of a Yorkshire butcher it merely reinforced the gap between the haves and the have nots.

Writing in his diaries, he said that his parents had taught him a few basic manners, such as tipping your soup bowl backwards, and he was shocked to find that the public school lot didn't seem to bother with table manners; they just got on and ate. His prejudices about the upper classes were confirmed when they started hurling pellets of bread at each other.

I was very sorry to hear that his first experience of the public school system should have proved such a disappointment. Alan, as I like to think of him, is not a lot older than I am, so it's not as if they were mates of Harry Flashman. A sense of entitlement has always been a feature of schools from the topmost drawers, and bread-throwing at mealtimes is not uncommon. But on the whole, the boys I met at my school and others like it had good manners and were rather modest about their place in the scheme of things.

Manners have never been part of any school curriculum: if they were taught at all, they were taught at home by parents. And in the absence of parents, by nannies.

They were the ones who told their children to sit up at the table and take their elbows off and not talk with their mouths full and eat what was on their plates. They also taught them to take their hands out of their pockets when talking to grown-ups, to stand up when any of them came into the room, and open doors for them, and to say 'please' and 'thank you', and to put their hands up over their mouths when coughing, and a handkerchief over their noses when sneezing.

Schools had their own rules for good behaviour. It was, for instance, polite to thank the captain of the house for giving you six of the best for forgetting to warm the lavatory seat for him.

Social behaviour one learnt largely by osmosis. Parents might offer the odd hint, but most of us learnt how to behave with girls at private dances, say, partly by observation, partly by stories passed on by sophisticated friends and partly by experience.

Though they rarely reaped any benefits, my friends and

I never failed to open doors for women of all ages, to walk on the outside of pavements, to write thank-you letters after dinner parties, and to leave a generous tip for the chambermaid after staying for a weekend in the country. Different people have different ways of defining good and bad manners. When at dinner, one friend of mine always leaves a little food on her plate ('for Mr Manners'); another dumped her long-standing boyfriend when he wrote to her parents thanking them for the weekend and sent it with a second-class stamp.

Time was when all bookshelves carried a volume or two on the subject of manners and etiquette. I have one called *Manners for Men* by Mrs Humphry (aka 'Madge' of *Truth*) which covers every last point of etiquette, from the correct way to address a duke to removing a cigar from one's mouth when passing ladies on the street or on the promenade.

It was published in 1897, when such things really mattered and rules of behaviour among certain sections of society were so arcane as to be risible. It was considered bad, for example, to sport anything other than a bowler hat in town until after Goodwood Week.

Evelyn Waugh made great fun of such 'immature taboos of dress' in *Put Out More Flags* when describing the schoolboyish Alastair Trumpington as war loomed and more and more friends started joining up:

'It came as a shock to him now to find his country at war and himself in pyjamas, spending his normal Sunday noon with a jug of Black Velvet and some chance visitors. Peter's uniform added to his uneasiness. It was as though he had been taken in adultery at Christmas or found in mid-June on the steps of Bratts in a soft hat.'

But then Alastair had devised his own, very personal code of conduct: 'Since marriage he had been unfaithful to Sonia for a week every year, during Bratts Club golf tournament at Le Touquet, usually with the wife of a fellow member. He did this without any scruple because he believed Bratts week to be in some way excluded from the normal life of loyalties and obligations; a Saturnalia when the laws did not run. At all other times he was a devoted husband.'

Etiquette may change with time and fashion, but manners will always matter, because good manners indicate kindness, of which there seems to be less and less in this self-absorbed, self-regarding world of social media.

I have tried to avoid giving my own children Polonial advice on anything – manners, behaviour, life in general – mainly because the lives of the young today are so very different from those heading for the old-age door. And because the world of my grandchildren is even further removed, I hesitate to offer more than words of encouragement – though I have to admit I have pitched in from time to time with suggestions as to how we might all feel a little more comfortable if they were to remove their elbows from the table.

When a particularly clever friend of mine arrived to take up his place at Oxford (something that would have been unimaginable for his parents), he commented to his tutor on how clever a fellow freshman was.

'Everyone here is clever,' said his tutor. 'The important thing is to be kind.'

In these times of ever stiffer competition and the constant demand for intellectual excellence, those might be useful words of wisdom for any grandfather to pass on to his grandchildren.

Very Feeble on the Rugger Field

As a grandfather, one struggles to know whether one should present oneself to one's grandson as a role model by exaggerating minor achievements on the playing field; warm acquaintance with celebrities one has only ever shaken hands with once; an intimate knowledge of the workings of high-performance motor cars, none of which one has ever been able to afford, etc, etc. Or should one go down the self-effacement route in the hope that it might help to boost any feelings of low self-esteem on his part?

Fortunately, the problem does not arise in the case of Ludo who, whatever his state of mind, always manages to have me on the back foot within moments of our meeting.

'Grandpa,' he said the other day, 'is it true that at school you were pretty much rubbish at games?'

'Well, I wouldn't go so far as to say I was—'

'Mummy said you were, and that you showed her some of your school reports, which said you were very feeble on the rugger field.'

I said that I had to admit it was not my natural game.

'What was, then?'

'I was a promising cricketer.'

'Batsman or bowler?'

'All-rounder,' I said.

'Were you in the First Eleven?'

'I wasn't in any teams, as such – unless you count the Haymakers.'

'The Haymakers?' he said with barely disguised scepticism.

'It was a scratch team we had at my school. For people who loved playing cricket but weren't good enough to get into any teams. We played against local villages. It was fun. We went with an Australian master called Digger Something and we were allowed to drink beer afterwards.'

'And smoke?'

'No smoking. But we had our own tie.'

'Cool.'

'Why are you so keen to know about my games record at school?'

'No reason,' he said.

But there was. I got a telephone call from my daughter the next day to say that Ludo was really upset at not being picked for the school junior rugger team, and would I have a reassuring word with him?

'I know you were no good at games at school, so you'll know what you're talking about,' she said.

For goodness' sake. There were some things I was good at. Latin, for example, and ... well, I can't be expected to remember every last detail of my academic life in the late forties; it was a very long time ago, and I went to quite a few schools in the years before I reached my teens.

It would be hard to imagine a more eccentric establishment than Llanabba Castle, the school in Wales where Paul Pennyfeather found employment after being sent down from Oxford for indecent behaviour. Or a man less suited to teaching boys than the great Captain Grimes. But my first prep school, in Surrey, ran it a close second.

The only real difference between them was that Llanabba was a creation of Evelyn Waugh's brilliant imagination, and mine was an actual school where seventy or so boys between the ages of seven and thirteen, including yours truly, were drilled in history and geography and French and maths by young men who were almost as egregious and in some cases close to being unhinged.

Finding anyone remotely suitable during and just after the war was a problem that many headmasters had to wrestle with, and it was the sheer exiguity of post-war talent that explained the bizarre assortment of types that graced the front row of the school photograph of summer 1949.

You had the feeling that they were glad to take on anyone who was fairly well educated and reasonably good with children – neither of which, it appeared, were essential qualifications for the job. When one of the maths masters lost his rag with a small boy and threw him out of a window, not only did the incident pass without comment from anyone present, or indeed from the boy's parents, but the man in question was kept on for the rest of the year.

Even as I was describing this to Ludo, I could sense incredulity.

I was beginning to wonder myself if I had imagined the whole thing.

He listened with a solemn look.

'That's really dangerous,' he said when I'd finished. 'He could have been really badly injured.'

'Actually,' I said, 'it was only a ground-floor window and luckily he landed in the herbaceous border.'

Having a grandson like Ludo can be daunting at times: not only is his knowledge of certain subjects far in advance of mine, but he rarely accepts any pronouncements I make at face value.

'The headmaster looks really nice,' Ludo said.

With his high domed forehead, bald head and round, tortoiseshell-framed glasses, he was a prep-school headmaster straight out of central casting.

'He looks quite old,' Ludo added.

'What do you mean by quite old?'

'About forty?'

'I think we all thought he was much older. His wife seemed to us boys to be older still. She wore a huge amount of make-up. In fact, a lot of the parents thought that was where most of the school fees went.'

'And did they?'

'Nothing would have surprised me about that school. The geography master used to come to school in an armoured car.'

Physical toughness was the keynote at all times – not a quality to which unconfident boys, like me, could easily aspire. Not when the cane was wielded as much as it was at that school, and dozens like it. Six of the best was the solution to the slightest misdemeanour.

No one ever complained, least of all the parents who believed that, whatever the circumstances, the school was always right.

'My father said that if I got six at school, I'd get six at home,' I said.

Ludo was outraged. 'He'd probably go to prison today.'

'My father?'

'The headmaster, anyway.'

'I was a day boy, luckily. You stood much more chance of getting beaten if you were a boarder. Once a boy got seen climbing a tree naked at midnight. Nobody would own up, so the entire dormitory was given six of the best. The boys had to cross the cricket field to get to the headmaster's study, where they were beaten one by one and came hobbling back, holding their bottoms. A friend of mine said that the event was invested with all the glamour of the Somme. Good for team spirit, though.'

'Did you ever get beaten, Grandpa?'

I hesitated. The answer was no. On the other hand, I had my *amour propre* to consider.

'There are worse punishments,' I said, 'than being whacked on the bottom. At least it's over and done with. For years I held a grudge against the captain of my house at my public school who caught me sending him up when I thought he wasn't looking.'

'What happened?'

'I got gated for a week – grounded, you'd call it – so I missed seeing the Australians playing Kent. I like to think I won the moral victory in the end.'

Even as I launched into the story I knew it wasn't the blood-stained Armageddon he was hoping for, but I pressed on anyway.

'I met him at a cricket match some years later. "What are you up to these days?" I enquired. "Still in lino," he said.'

I was anxious and fearful as a child, and as a seventy-eight-year-old I am even more so. I realise that almost everyone who turns his hand to autobiography these days seizes the opportunity to claim some weakness of character. Anxiety, timidity and fear of physical violence are high on many writers' lists of childhood failings. Possibly to make themselves seem more interesting and to curry sympathy from their readers. In my case, I have the written evidence – thanks entirely to my mother.

For some reason best known to herself, she kept all my school reports. I mean *all* my school reports – from my very first term at my kindergarten, aged five, until the day I left my public school thirteen years later. I found them after she died and they make uncomfortable reading, even after all these years. But if they helped in any way to ease Ludo's anxieties and suggest that he was not alone in being not quite as good at games as some, I could see no reason not to share some of them with him.

We began with the general report for Christmas term 1948. I was only nine, but there were already strong hints that I was going to have to pull my socks up if I wanted to impress on the rugger field.

Ludo started reading out comments at random. "'His rugger is rather on the feeble side. He must make up his mind to try harder and not think so much about the hard knocks." "Still a nonentity on the rugger pitch." "He is not a natural competitor ... "'

'Yes, well, I think we've got the point, Ludo,' I said. But the bit was well and truly between the teeth.

"'He is *very* feeble on the rugger field." "I wish he'd show more life on the rugger field. I'm tired of seeing him standing in his overcoat on the touch line, though it is a very nice overcoat."'

'Ah,' I said. 'That was after I'd had a rather nasty operation and was off games. But at that school, there was no such thing as off games. Not even after a nasty operation.'

Of course he wanted to know what the operation was for, but there are some things a grandfather prefers to keep to himself and this was one of them. Not that that deterred him from pressing on with yet more damaging material.

'Does not like rugger when it's wet and cold.' Ludo paused, then he said, 'No one likes rugger when it's wet and cold.'

'Some clearly do.' I pointed at the headmaster's report for Christmas term 1948.

'"The liking for a muddy rugger ground and a punch on the nose in the boxing ring will come in time." I didn't know you did boxing at school, Grandpa.'

'Not just me. Everyone did. I don't mean everyone had boxing lessons. You could do boxing once a week but very few did. But when it came to the house boxing competition in the Christmas term, every boy was expected to take part. And not merely expected. Compelled.'

'Even if you hadn't boxed before in your life?'

'Especially if you hadn't boxed before in your life.'

'How could you box if you didn't know how to?'

It was a question I asked the master who took boxing (as an alternative to rugger, though not in my view a very attractive one) on the days when he wasn't teaching maths. I went further and suggested that if a boy who didn't know how to box was picked to fight a boy who did, it would be an unfair contest and rather a pointless one.

He gave me the sort of look I imagine Mr Bumble must have given Oliver Twist when he asked for a second helping of gruel.

'"God, you're wet," said the master. "Have you no loyalty to your house? Or to your school? Stand up straight, boy. Oh, I'd forgotten; you can't. You haven't got a backbone."'

Ludo said, 'You could have asked your mother to write a letter to the headmaster saying you didn't have to box because you were a conscientious objector.'

I said that I wouldn't have been let off if I'd been the next incarnation of the Dalai Lama, and that the worst thing any boy could do in those days was to be shown up as a coward. Or, rather, even more of a coward than I clearly was in the eyes of most male members of staff.

'You could have said you weren't feeling well.'

I explained that no excuses, however drastic, were accepted when it came to the boxing competition. If I had come in with one arm in plaster I would have ended up boxing one-handed. Unfortunately, I had been picked against a boy called Harness. No one wanted to face him and I knew I couldn't win; no one ever had. He was quite a nice chap, actually. Just much bigger than everyone else of his age.

During the previous afternoon, all the chairs in the assembly hall had been stacked up and the tables arranged in the rough shape of a boxing ring. The expression 'on the ropes' had especially uncomfortable associations

I couldn't eat any macaroni cheese at lunch, and by the time the boxing competition started at three o'clock my mouth was drier than the Gobi Desert. Harness looked bigger than ever in his vest and shorts. The gym teacher, who was the referee, helped me on with a pair of gloves that were sticky with blood from the previous bout.

'Good luck, lad,' he said. 'Just remember to keep your guard up.' That was it. I had to do something so, as Harness and I were about to go on, I said that if I promised not to hit him hard, would he promise not to hit me hard back?

'Okay,' he said.

'Don't forget,' I whispered as we touched gloves in the middle of the ring.

'Right-oh,' he said, and the next thing I knew he'd punched me on the nose so hard that my eyes immediately filled with tears and I couldn't see a thing. I waved my arms about help-lessly while Harness pulverised me.

After what seemed like half an hour but was probably no more than half a minute, the referee stopped the bout.

Harness raised both arms above his head like an old-fashioned prize fighter while I stood there, my face covered in blood, tears and shame.

I thought, I'll never recover from this. Any hopes I might have of winning a cup, or getting into a team, or seeing my name on an honours board had gone for ever. The next thing I knew, the headmaster was pumping my hand and congratu-lating me on a gutsy performance. 'Say not the struggle naught availeth,' he declaimed. 'The labour and the wounds are vain.'

Well, they didn't seem very vain to me.

Ludo said, 'Is that from a poem?'

'Arthur Hugh Clough, 1849.'

'What does it mean?'

'It means don't give up, even though you're being beaten to pulp, because it will all come right in the end.'

'Oh,' he said.

I said, 'It's like you and rugger. Never give up.'

'It's all very well saying that, Grandpa,' said Ludo, 'but first you've got to get into the team, and I haven't been picked for one.'

It crossed my mind to lighten his mood by mentioning that I once played cricket for the Oxford University Dramatic Society against the Royal Shakespeare Company at Stratford. The only reason we won was because their fielders all brought their beer on with them and never managed to stop a ball because it took too long to put their glasses down before they started running.

On the other hand, I could see that I was worse at sports psychology than I had been at rugger and boxing, so instead we went out and had a burger, which cheered both of us no end.

Bucket List Bonanza

'What you need are some hobbies.'

Can there be any words guaranteed to send a bigger chill down the spine of every seventy-something-year-old who thinks he's forty? Could there be a more depressing thought than that of a cheerless room full of ancient individuals in ill-fitting gym clothes being shouted at by an aerobics teacher? Or shuffling round a makeshift dance floor in a geriatric foxtrot? Or dreaming of being another Winston Churchill with paints and easel in a sunny square in Marrakech while sitting in an evening class for beginners, struggling to draw a bowl of apples?

Some years ago I spent a morning at my grandson's kindergarten, where I ended up lowering myself nervously in the direction of a tiny stool, like a circus elephant, after which the two of us were presented with tubs of differently shaped pieces of plastic, out of which we were expected to make Picassoesque images.

I quickly found myself at sea and, before I had a chance to make a creative move, the teacher was leaning over me, offering me simple hints. 'Now if you were put this one here and that one there ... doesn't that look just like a house?'

I said that as a training tool for life in an old people's home it was unbeatable.

'Don't give up,' she said. 'Look, Ludo's just made a dinosaur.'

Had I been blessed with a nanogram of artistic talent, I can't believe it wouldn't have revealed itself years ago. Possibly at my nursery school.

Late last year I came across a feature in one of the posh Sundays entitled '50 things for the over-50s to do'. 'New research,' it said, 'proves that mid-lifers are ideally equipped for new challenges and opportunities. Such as these ... ' And there followed four pages of what might loosely be called hobbies.

You might say that lumping oneself in with mid-lifers at the age of seventy-eight is tempting ridicule. On the other hand, as I think I may have mentioned, I am happy in the belief that I am currently enjoying late middle age; and cliché though it may be, one really is only as young as one feels. Skimming through the list of things I 'can, should, and must do in part two of my life', I was enormously cheered to find several which, even if I didn't immediately turn to the websites in question, I felt sure I could do.

Some were clearly not suitable, or even possible. Running for political office, for example (though President Trump is a fellow septuagenarian and Ronald Reagan was my age when he left the White House); or becoming an Olympian, or a magistrate, or a zoo keeper. Others I have already tackled at some stage, with varying degrees of success.

Though you would never know it to see me at a wedding,

standing on a dance floor, gyrating gently in an embarrassing OAP version of the twist, that I actually do know how to ballroom dance. My reverse turn in the quickstep was much admired at teenage dances in the fifties, and though the paso doble and the tango were as far beyond my capabilities then as they would be now, my somewhat agricultural rhumba was legendary in East Surrey.

I have also written a novel or two, and once took up fencing at school. Indeed, I was appointed captain of fencing for my house and could, I still believe, have led my team to glory had I not come up against a boy who threw such training as he had acquired out of the window and launched himself at me like Ronald Colman in *The Prisoner of Zenda*.

Those aside, there are a number of suggestions that appeal.

For as long as I can remember I have regretted that I never learnt to fly – and guess what: there is no upper age limit for a private pilot's licence in the UK, though passing the medical might be a bridge too far.

It's unlikely that I could follow in the footsteps of JK Simmons, who had to wait years until he finally found stardom at the age of the nearly sixty, winning an Oscar, a Golden Globe and a Bafta as the sadistic music teacher in *Whiplash*. On the other hand, it would seem that elderly fashion models of both sexes are in demand – though I would have to draw the line if it came to parading bare-chested in front of the likes of Dame Anna Wintour.

Should I sign up for the marathon, perhaps? I'm always reading about ancient individuals who raise money for a good cause and are still slogging on bravely long after everyone has gone home.

However, as a schoolboy I always associated going for a run with punishment – often for some trivial misdemeanour – so the idea of running for pleasure or profit could never have been further from my mind.

Anyway . . . twenty-six *miles*?

Missing from the list of challenges and opportunities to keep the older away from the daytime television screen and the armchair are two of the best loved and most popular, namely golf and bridge.

Should anyone reading this be thinking of ways of arming him or herself against the empty spaces of old age, they could do worse than learn how to swing a golf club in such a way that it connects with a ball sufficiently well that it enables them to enjoy countless healthy hours of walking in attractive countryside in congenial company.

For further thoughts on golf, the chapter entitled 'In The Bunker!' might help to persuade you one way or the other.

And then there's bridge.

I am less qualified to express an opinion on the benefits of this hugely popular, challenging and stimulating game/hobby/occupation/entertainment/ passion/way of life for one very good reason, and that is that I don't play bridge.

I know what you're asking yourself, and you won't be the last to ask it: how in the world did this apparently well brought up, educated, socially acceptable and intelligent man get as far as he has done in the world without once playing bridge? It is surely one of those skills that every young man who wishes to have a hope of getting on in society needs to have in his locker, along with riding, tennis, croquet, small talk and opening an oyster.

Don't think I haven't considered taking bridge lessons. My wife, who has been a passionate and, by all accounts, a handy bridge player for more than fifty years, was keen at one time that I should become a member of Andrew Robson's famous Bridge Club and learn at the hands of a master. However, any hopes she might have had of transforming me from a card-playing dunce into something worthy of being her regular partner were dashed when we discovered that the French woman who lived two doors away happened to be a bridge teacher. Meeting at a drinks party, I mentioned the possibility of taking up the game, assuming that she would give the project an enthusiastic thumbs-up, if not offer to teach me herself. I could not have been more mistaken.

'No, no, no,' she said firmly, like a Gallic Mrs Thatcher. 'It is not possible for a husband and wife to play bridge together; not if the wife is a good player and the husband is a beginner. That can only lead to divorce, if not murder.'

I discovered exactly what she meant when she (Mrs Matthew, I mean) tried to introduce me to backgammon and I drove her nearly demented by moving my checkers at the speed of a three-year-old at nursery school and counting the numbers out loud as I did so.

Not that even she is a stranger to the slings, arrows and tongue-lashings hurled across the green baize by over-competitive players of every stripe.

On board a cruise ship in the deepest Caribbean, Mrs Matthew set off cheerfully to try her hand at what was described as 'advanced bridge'. She had been gone barely half an hour when she was back, white and shaken, having been crushed under the heel (or should that be hand?) of a terrifying American woman who treated her bridge partners as ruthlessly as an income tax inspector with a large dash of hyena blood in him.

If that can happen to an experienced player, what must it be like for a beginner? All pastimes should be fun and diverting, not some form of adult torture.

As Peter Cook once said of the theatre, 'I go to be entertained. I don't want to see plays about rape, sodomy and drug addiction. I can get all that at home.'

Song and Dance

In 1974 I spent an evening in London talking golf and much else with Alistair Cooke. He was staying in a flat in Mount Street, and I was editing a travel magazine for *The Times*. Having seen the success that the then editor of *Punch*, Bill Davis, had had with *High Life* (the British Airways in-flight magazine that he had founded and was editing at the same time), largely as a result of employing well-known names such as Frederick Forsyth, Harry Secombe, Alan Whicker and Harold Wilson, I decided I could do a lot worse than follow his example.

Having learned that Alistair Cooke was in town, I rang him to ask if he would be prepared to write a piece on great golf courses he had played here and in America.

He would be delighted, he said. Would I come round to his flat at six-thirty and we could have a chat about it?

Though only in his mid-sixties at the time, his hair was white and he looked older and stooped a little for a man of his age. He had only recently finished filming his great documentary series, *America*, and when he described the punishing schedule, I understood why.

'I hope you drink whisky,' he said. There is always some-thing unreal about meeting someone of enormous fame, especially if you have known his voice on the wireless since he first started *Letter from America* when I was a small boy and listened to him – often uncomprehendingly – on my parents' large walnut-veneered radiogram.

Not only was it his voice that was so familiar, but so too was his way of approaching any subject by coming at it sideways rather than head on. He did exactly the same that evening, answering questions I put to him by speaking about some-thing totally different and working his way effortlessly and elegantly towards his answer.

We had been chatting for a short time when his wife, Jane, popped her head round the door to say she was just off and would see him later. He explained that she was going to a special ballet performance at the London Coliseum in honour of a pair of Israeli dancers – the Panovs – who had managed, with enormous difficulty, to emigrate from Russia to Israel and en route were giving their last performance in Europe and wanted to thank their fans in England for their support.

I asked him why he wasn't going too. He said he had never cared for the ballet and was too old to start taking up new interests of that kind.

I wondered at the time, and have often wondered since, if one is ever too old to acquire a taste for such things – be it ballet, opera, theatre, art exhibitions, whatever.

I have been particularly guilty of not taking the opportuni-ties when they have occurred, which they have, in the shape of weekly visits with a top-flight expert to every single important arts exhibition in town that Mrs Matthew and several of her girlfriends have been attending for many years now. I can't explain why I've been so loath to join in. The women who go are all very affable, and they seem to have a very jolly time, meeting for coffee beforehand and a big end-of-term lunch three times a year.

Could it just be because I'd be the only bloke? And why should that be a matter of concern, since I would be going to look at pictures and learn about them, not to be some object of curiosity? When I do sometimes go to exhibitions which they have all been to and have recommended, I have never been disappointed.

Abstract art had always been to me a particular mystery that I had no immediate plans to solve, until a friend of mine, an RA no less, invited me to join him for a visit to the big abstract expressionism show at the Royal Academy. It helped enormously that I went round it one evening after closing time and in the company of a man who was able not only to educate me in who these painters were and how and where and why the movement started, but also to open my eyes to a style of painting to which they had hitherto been firmly closed.

However, like Alistair Cooke, I have a feeling that ballet will remain the mystery to me that it has always been. As a journalist on the inaugural flight of Concorde to Moscow in 1985 (a rather longer one than I'd imagined because the plane was not permitted to fly supersonically anywhere except over the sea), I joined my fellow passengers at a performance of *Don Quixote* at the Bolshoi which I don't remember at all, and, more recently, Mrs M and I had a very jolly evening at a performance of *The Nutcracker* at the Mariinsky in St Petersburg, but balletomania did not strike on either occasion, and I have not been since.

I can't pretend that opera has loomed large in my cultural landscape either. I have always suspected that, like so many tastes, it needs to be acquired early. Leave it until later and one is not equipped with that lifetime of experiences in opera houses great and small all over the world that allows full enjoyment of a performance.

Having said that, I have a lurking suspicion that, of all the performing arts, a taste for opera might be all the more rewarding when acquired later in life.

One person who discovered it in his sixties was John Mortimer, whose keen eye for the pretentious was never keener than when surrounded by the well-to-do, for whom opera and ballet are an essential accompaniment to corporate life.

While standing in the Crush Bar in the Royal Opera House, enjoying a glass of champagne before a performance of some much-lauded opera, he heard a man who had obviously arrived later than expected and slightly panic-stricken saying to his wife, 'What are they giving us tonight, darling? Singing or dancing?'

I suspect that all the big opera venues are heavily populated by such types, though I'm glad to say that I didn't spot anyone like that on a glorious afternoon last year when a very kind friend introduced us to Wagner, in the shape of *Die Meistersinger von Nürnberg* at Glyndebourne.

Never would I have believed that I could sit for nearly five hours, completely entranced by music which, apart from the overture, I had never heard before, in a language that I didn't speak, and with a story that I didn't know. Watching the final scene with more singers and dancers than I would have believed possible to fit on a stage, I felt like a small child seeing a giant firework display for the first time and being taken through the world's biggest toy shop all rolled into one.

For that one summer's day alone I will remember our friend with affection and gratitude, tinged with some sadness that I have spent a life missing so much.

It is also a matter of great regret to me that I did not persist with my piano lessons when I was at school. I can think up any number of reasons why I didn't. At fifteen, I had more amusing things to do with my free time than sit in a gloomy little room, practising my scales. Remembering that my repertoire never advanced beyond a stumbling version of 'Dolly's Funeral', and knowing that it never will, I can only curse myself for not acquiring even the most basic skills for what might have been a lasting joy to me in my old age.

Not only was I lazy; I was far too impatient. I wanted to learn to play stuff, not practise it. There was a boy at my prep school who, at the age of eleven, was able to play the piano by ear. I don't mean he could knock off the Moonlight Sonata after listening to it once: his style was based on that of Charlie Kunz, a natty-looking dance band leader and pianist with a little moustache whose tinkling tones were often to be heard dancing across the ground floor of our little house in Surrey in the fifties: 'You're Breaking My Heart', 'C'est Si Bon', 'Unforgettable', that kind of stuff.

'Can you play "Walking My Baby Back Home", Barry?' someone would ask this boy and he would. Straight off, just like that. It was if Charlie himself were sitting there in the front of us. Uncanny.

I imagined that within a couple of weeks of starting lessons with the piano teacher assigned to me at school, my
own fingers would be flying across the keys, and that a brisk
performance of a Kunzian piano medley by me during break
every day would be an essential ingredient of school life. But
'Dolly's Funeral'?

I could have stuck at it, and I should have done. But all was
not lost. At my next school, in Canterbury, I was accepted into
the choir and I continued to sing for the next five years – not
just in that, but also in the school choral society.

Indeed, in the summer of 1956 I appeared on stage as
a Gentleman of Japan in a production of *The Mikado*. My
early passion for greasepaint, acquired ten years earlier when
playing Third Shepherd in the local church nativity play, was
fully satisfied when I saw myself for the first time in kimono,
pigtailed wig and extravagant eyebrows, holding a fan and
looking oddly like Grayson Perry.

But I wasn't very musical. What am I saying? I wasn't
musical at all.

Luckily, I made friends with one or two boys who had been
at the Cathedral Choir School, so as long as I stood next to
one of them I was able to follow their lead and learn various
scores, and so lend my reedy tenor to lusty performances
of the *Messiah*, *Judas Maccabeus* and Hubert Parry's 'I was
Glad'.

The day I left school marked the end of my choral career.
Well, not completely. About thirty years ago a friend of ours
used to invite a gang of people to an early Christmas party
which involved singing in the Scratch *Messiah* at the Albert
Hall, followed by grub and gargle back at his place.

Surrounded by seven thousand amateur choristers (many of them carrying the weight of many decades and some of them entire choirs) and led by a top-class orchestra under the baton of the redoubtable Sir David Willcocks – a small figure in a white jacket who, from where we used to sit, was just about visible without the aid of binoculars – it was unlikely that any sounds that issued from my mouth were going to add or detract from the general swell of sound that arose when the entire place rose to its feet in the Hallelujah Chorus.

Indeed, it didn't really matter whether one sang or not: just to be there, looking out over a full Albert Hall and listening to the whole place in full throat, was enough in itself to set the pulse racing.

Nothing could possibly go wrong. Or could it? There is a moment of total silence between the penultimate and the very last Amen, and every year I wondered if someone, in their enthusiasm, might one day misread the score and add an extra Amen to the proceedings. Worse still, that that one might be me.

Those evenings were my definitive choral swansongs, and despite enthusiastic urging from Mrs Matthew to join the two choirs she sings in, I feel that there is little likelihood of my career being revived.

Several of my friends also sing the praises of joining a choir, and the joy on Mrs M's face and those of her fellow members is palpable as they join in another stirring chorus from the *St Matthew Passion* or the Brahms *Requiem*. But for me, not being able to read music could prove to be a problem.

'Anyone wishing to join is welcome,' the conductor of my wife's choir announced in a bid to recruit new members following a thrilling performance of *Carmina Burana*. 'No one need be backward in coming forward. There is no audition. Everyone can sing.'

Well, there are always exceptions to every rule, and I am one of them. Even at carol services I can do little more than mouth the words in a low monotone. These days I seem increasingly to have Van Gogh's ear for music.

The eternally youthful Gareth Malone has proved over and over again that it is possible, given sufficient will and determination, to draw gold from base metal, and I know a conductor of a choir who once a week will hold sessions for members who can't read music and can't really sing, and she says that some of them get on quite well. But with the best will in the world, I would not want her or anyone else's professional time to be spent trying to get musical blood out of a tone-deaf stone.

The sad thing for me is that almost everyone I speak to seems to be in a choir somewhere these days – especially people of my age. Given the huge number that have been established in recent years, we who are not able to turn down unappealing dinner invitations with the excuse that we are very sorry but we have a rehearsal for Haydn's *Nelson Mass* that evening might soon find ourselves in a minority.

Many of those who join do so not because they enjoy singing so much as the conviviality that is part and parcel of the weekly rehearsals, and there are always a handful who feel sure that no one will mind if they miss most of them and just turn up on the day of the performance.

Could there be anything more irritating to a dedicated choir member who has checked in to rehearsals week after week and practised hard at home to turn up for the performance only to find that her regular seat is occupied by complete stranger? Or, worse still, that the seat in front has been taken by a choral cuckoo in the nest?

The people who make a habit of this are, I understand from such research as I have carried out on the subject, largely women, and the women in question are nearly always large, thereby making it almost impossible for the normal-sized regular to see the conductor.

Not every choir will tolerate such a laissez-faire attitude. One choir mistress I spoke to on this thorny subject said, 'A lot of our eighty-five choir members are rather elderly and some of those come along just to have a coffee and a chat with their friends – often when they're not supposed to. We have a strict rule that if you're not good enough to sing in the concert you can't come for the three weeks beforehand. We need to have good rehearsals.'

Mind you, she is an old hand in the choir business: young conductors, faced with an array of hardened and determined old stagers, could well have much of their valuable time cut out making sure they know who's boss.

To judge from a secret dossier passed to me recently by a maestro who would never stand any nonsense from any member, however senior, all too many methods have been devised by singers set on establishing their preferred pecking order.

This unofficial guide to keeping a conductor in his place lists no less than seventeen ploys. Here is a brief selection:

Remember to bury your head in your score just before the conductor gives you your cues.

Always clear your throat loudly during pauses. Quiet instrumental interludes are the perfect opportunity for blowing your nose very loudly.

Wait until well into the rehearsal before letting the conductor know that you don't have the music.

If you are singing in a language with which the conductor is even the tiniest bit unfamiliar, make sure to ask as many questions as possible about the meaning of individual words. If this fails, enquire about the correct pronunciation of the most difficult ones.

Ask, as casually as possible, if the conductor happens to have heard the von Karajan recording of the piece.

During a long and very meaningful rest, either hold the previous note a second too long, or come in a beat before the rest is over.

The document concludes with the following piece of advice:

Make every effort to take the attention away from the podium and put it on you, where it rightly belongs.

The more I hear about the joys of choral life, the more I wonder whether it really is too late to try to find that youthful tenor voice that has been lost for so long. Indeed, has it really been lost at all, and in my old age, will it suddenly be miraculously restored like the blind man's sight in Mark 8:25? I feel more and more that I am missing out on one of the greatest pleasures of old age.

I suppose I could just turn up each week and *pretend* to sing. I wouldn't be alone – as I know, having sat in many of the concerts in which Mrs M has taken part and had ample time to examine the faces of every one of the choir members in action. Or not, as the case may be. I know exactly who the guilty ones are. My only worry is that someone might be sitting there with their beady eyes focused on *me*.

It's Hardly What You'd Call Man's Work

Old age may have all manner of pleasures up its sleeve for me as I head into my late seventies, but one of them will almost certainly not be standing on the deck of a cruise liner with Mrs Matthew at my side, both dressed in our smart casual best, gazing across an azure ocean at yet another perfect sunset with glasses of light white wine in our hands.

I know this for one very good reason: we once went on a cruise round the Caribbean, and for all the jolly on-board entertainments and diversions, and excursions to exotic islands, and drinks parties, and jokes, we both agreed that that was to be our first cruise and our last: at least of the sort that the elegant couples you see standing on the decks of cruise liners in newspaper travel supplements go on.

Not that there were any on that particular occasion – or, anyway, none that we came across. Our liner was part of a large fleet and carried something in the region of two thousand passengers – though sometimes it seemed a lot more.

It was probably my wife's experience at the advanced bridge morning, as described earlier, that was the nail in the cruising coffin for her – though to be fair to the cruise line, she has never been a fan of life on the ocean wave, and didn't altogether endear herself to the Captain at his drinks party by constantly referring to his 70,000-ton liner as 'your boat'.

(Mind you, she had rather put her foot in it within moments of boarding by mistaking him for the Entertainments Officer.)

Given that I was there, along with a variety of hacks, at the invitation of the cruise-line company, to write about the food on and off the ship for *Vogue* magazine, and thus at no financial cost to ourselves, we decided to count ourselves lucky and treat our ten days at sea for all the world as if we were pukka, fully paid-up passengers.

We certainly threw ourselves into the proceedings as if we were.

One of our colleagues, a seasoned travel writer and editor, came with a dazzling wardrobe of cruise wear and tales of encounters with Noël Coward, Cecil Beaton and the Queen Mother. Never for a moment did he give the impression that he was anything other than completely at home, breakfasting on the upper deck in silk shirt and immaculate white ducks, with shoes to match.

I did my best to mirror his air of elegant insouciance until one day, as we were leaning over the ship's rail staring out over yet another perfect blue sea and identical sky, he turned to me and said, 'I don't know about you, but I feel this is hardly what you'd call man's work.'

That was thirty years ago. Would I go on a cruise again? Not with Mrs M, of course, but on my own? Probably not. Not even if it was a freebie from start to finish? Hmmm. What if it was a genuinely luxurious cruise? Or if I were a guest speaker?

Those ten days aboard the *Sea Princess* in the Caribbean in the eighties were not what you'd call luxury cruising of the sort that many of my friends have enjoyed in great style from the South Seas and the Norwegian Fjords to the Classical Mediterranean and the Antarctic. As a reward for a lifetime of hard work, they assure me that nothing beats a top-class cruise with like-minded people – preferably not too many of them at a time.

The more expensive and exclusive the cruise, the more likely it is that the average age of the passenger list is in the high sixties if not the seventies.

We have a friend, well into her eighties, who is a keen cruiser, but who goes to enormous lengths to give similarly old passengers the widest possible berth – on the grounds that she finds the younger ones better company in every possible way.

Not surprisingly, perhaps, there are many younger passengers who will go to similar lengths. One seasoned cruiser told me that the trick is to keep a wary eye out for 'no-fly cruises' which are much favoured by elderly passengers who have got to the stage when they feel they can no longer cope with the aggravation, uncertainty and general chaos of airports and prefer to board directly from Southampton and similar ports of departure.

His principal complaint about them is not just that they always take so long to get everywhere, and hold up queues for the self-service buffet and monopolise the lifts, but that they all read the *Daily Telegraph*.

Not, he added, that one can avoid them altogether. Single ladies of advanced years are part of the warp and woof of cruising life. A seventy-something devotee of life on the bounding main let me into the secret of why so many of his contemporaries enjoy a world that only cruise ships can provide.

'They love being surrounded by servants,' he explained, 'all of them ready to hurry forward and take an order for a second glass of champagne. It gives them the illusion of grandeur and a glimpse of the past.'

Elderly female passengers may have different, more secret, motives.

'Undoubtedly there are people who go because they expect to fall in love on a cruise,' another regular told me. 'A lot of ladies go to find romance, if only with the second officer. But it doesn't often happen in real life. I remember one crew member telling me that, as single, unattached ladies approach the end of the voyage and realise that the only handsome stranger they're going to meet is a customs officer, the drinking can become quite ferocious.'

One old boy who arrived hoping for some late-life hanky panky confided this to a fellow passenger who had already been on board for nearly a week and enquired in a conspiratorial voice if he had had any luck. 'Good Lord, yes,' said the man. 'Every day, so far.'

I'm wondering whether he might be related to the Earl of Warwick, with whom the late Marjorie Proops once became engaged on a cruise to the West Indies, as she explained on a programme about travel I once chaired on Radio 4.

The story went that she was introduced to this aristocratic figure by somebody in the bar, at which he declared, 'I have loved you from afar for twenty years. Will you marry me?'

She suggested they might sit down and have a drink, and think about it, and get to know each other a bit over a vodka and tonic.

'Is that what you like to drink?' he asked. She said that it was, whereupon he shouted 'Jean Jacques!' (The waiter's name was Rousseau.) 'Bring a large vodka and tonic for my fiancée, Mrs Proops!'

He continued to refer to her in this way for the rest of the voyage, and it must have come as quite a surprise to fellow passengers, some of whom felt they knew her as well as any member of their own family and were conscious that she was holidaying on her own, to discover that she was about to join the aristocracy.

On the night of the Captain's Gala, when everyone on board dressed in their gladdest rags and, in some cases, their best jewellery, Marje put on her favourite paste brooch. A woman at the same table turned up in emeralds.

The earl was very taken by these and, having admired them, turned to Marje and said, 'And where are your jewels?'

She replied that she was wearing them.

He said, in loud and lordly tones, 'The day you become my bride, I shall cover you in diamonds and rubies and give you the world.' She thanked him very much and told him to get on with his dinner, it was getting cold.

Mr Proops was waiting for her when they reached Southampton. She introduced him to her new husband, and the two of them became great friends on the spot.

The only downside of this brief, illusory and altogether eccentric on-board romance was when a gossip column in a daily newspaper (not the *Mirror*) announced that Marjorie

Proops was to become the next Countess of Warwick.

But then, of course, not every single lady over seventy steps aboard a liner determined to find late-life love – not least because of the very real danger of becoming something of a lame duck.

I heard of one eighty-year-old who spent her entire life on cruise ships, getting off one at some port or other and then getting on to another, no matter where it was going. When asked why, she explained that she had been widowed for many years and her family had their own lives and didn't want her around, and so she lived on ships where everyone was kind to her.

I understand from a certain matronly cruise aficionada that one way of ensuring that you look as if you are already the object of huge affection and are far from being unloved and unwanted is by ascending the gangplank carrying an armful of flowers. Once settled, you can set about doing what you always do – namely sitting alone in a deck chair staring at the sea or the sky or both. Others in search of blissful solitude spend their days walking round the deck.

Many, though, will take advantage of the myriad on-board entertainments and activities – gourmet cookery, wine tasting, salsa dancing, deck quoits, bridge, mini-golf, whatever.

That one cruise we were on offered a touch or two of culture in the shapes of an extremely good, if rather gloomy, pianist from Yorkshire who gave a couple of concerts and chaired a musical quiz, and a man who dressed up as Charles Dickens and in the middle of the morning while most were out on the deck or in the pool, recited chunks of *Great Expectations*. The theatre was far from full.

But ours was not what you'd call a cultural cruise. Retired folk with an urge to catch up on their long-forgotten education – given that they had any in the first place – will always find there are plenty of voyages on offer to suit their tastes, with interesting lectures by distinguished academics and occasional entertainments by well-known TV personalities.

Indeed, the mere rumour that Gregg Wallace, say, is on board can provide some passengers with days of entertainment as they scour the decks in the hope of encountering the cheery face and the shiny dome in person.

Flipping through a selection of themed cruises being offered in recent years by the likes of Swan Hellenic, Voyages to Antiquity and Noble Caledonian, my eye was caught by Classical Music in the Norwegian Fjords, Murder and Mystery, Links and Lobster in New England (that's lobster-tasting and golf lessons), Archimedes and Science in the Classical World, and even an *Archers*-themed cruise (as in Ambridge rather than Agincourt).

A friend of mine once went on a Russian cruise and found himself at a detailed lecture on the Russian health service – something he had not expected in over twenty years of ploughing the high seas. He said it was one of the most interesting two hours he'd spent in many a year, though when asked to give a flavour of it, was unable to remember a single thing.

Not Watching Television

A few years ago I did a radio series with Des Lynam called *Touchline Tales*, in which we travelled to minor sporting events not too far away from where we live. We watched tennis at Eastbourne and cricket at the Oval and went racing at Goodwood and wandered around, chatting, reminiscing, swapping anecdotes, telling jokes, forgetting what it was we were talking about, and generally doing what old geezers do on day outings.

It was while we were at Blackheath Golf Club that I asked for his advice on a subject that had been niggling at me for some time, and to which I hoped he would give me his whole-hearted support. I said that whenever my wife finds me watching golf or rugger or tennis on television she always makes some comment to the effect that I watch too much television in the afternoons.

I say that I am not 'watching television' as such, I am watching a rugger match/tennis match/golf competition on television, which is quite different. Were I lucky enough to have acquired tickets for the event in question, or rich enough to afford to travel to Augusta, or Melbourne or wherever, I would at that moment be there. Instead, I am making the best of it and watching it on the television. I am watching sport on television; I am not watching television.

Des said, 'I don't see the difference. There's you, there's the television and you're watching it. That's what's generally known as watching television.'

I'd like to think that he knew exactly what I was getting at and was in full sympathy, but one can never be too sure with Des. He likes nothing better than having a little harmless fun at one's expense. That's an Irish upbringing for you.

Don't misunderstand me; I have nothing against people watching television whenever they feel like. If you have nothing else on the cards, *Countdown* is a perfectly respectable way of passing three-quarters of an hour of a quiet afternoon. Anagrams are as good a recipe for keeping the old loaf alive as any, and I have heard of several distinguished writers and academics who are fans. I have never been able to fathom the numbers game, but some of the words that nice Susie Dent comes up with in Dictionary Corner are really quite educational.

Where I do draw the line is *Gogglebox*. Sitting on my sofa watching other people sitting on their sofas watching television programmes that I haven't watched and would not have chosen and making inane comments about them is akin to my worst nightmare – to wit, that I might one day find myself (given that I have enough brain left to be aware of anything) sitting in the lounge of an old people's home surrounded by old people, all staring mindlessly at television programmes that I wouldn't have chosen and making inane comments about them.

I'd feel as if I were in a remake of *One Flew Over the Cuckoo's Nest*, being permanently kept under the unforgiving thumb and tranquilising drugs of an English version of Nurse Ratched.

If one is destined to end one's days in a home, let it be like the one Diana Athill lives in.

Following a long and distinguished career in publishing with André Deutsch, she turned to writing and has produced more than half a dozen glorious volumes of memoirs, of which one of the best known is *Somewhere Towards the End* which came out in 2008. Anyone who wants to have some idea of what it's like to be old need look no further.

Reflecting, largely without regret, on the loves, friendships and events of her long life, Miss Athill considers the losses and gains that old age bring, and cheerfully offers wonderfully wise thoughts as she contemplates the prospect of her demise.

Now fast approaching her hundredth birthday, she lives – as she has done for the last few years – in a small room in a residential home in North London, surrounded by her books, a few pieces of her own furniture and the warmth and friendship of like-minded fellow residents.

She is the first to admit that she is very lucky: she is able to lead as independent a life as anyone of her advanced age could hope for, and for a long time would venture out on short expeditions in her own car.

In an interview given to the *Guardian* in 2015 she described how, when lying awake at night, she lets her imagination wander as she revisits the past, often running through all the men she ever went to bed with – which must, by her own account, occupy many a long stretch as her body waits for sleep.

Sometimes, she admits, she embroiders the past by telling herself stories of what might have happened, but dismisses this as 'a lazy exercise of the imagination' and considers it to be 'rather senile'.

She does not, as so many do at a great age, feel time dragging. On the contrary. 'The days whizz by,' she says. 'The older you get, the quicker the time goes. Odd, that.'

This sensation is not peculiar to the very old. Everyone, from middle age onwards, notices it – though in my experience the days seem to go by at roughly the same speed they always did; it's the weeks and months that flash by. Birthdays come round with particularly alarming speed, as does Christmas. The sensation of one's fingers on rough bark is so instantly familiar that one could swear it was only a week ago that one was last putting up the tree.

There is a scientific explanation for all this, which I hesitate to propound in detail, mainly because I don't really understand it. Neither, it seems, do the scientists. It would appear that there is no area in the human brain that deals with time perception. Our body clock governs our circadian rhythms, but has nothing whatsoever to do with our estimation of the passing of minutes, hours and years.

The simple answer may be that because, as we get older, we have fewer new experiences and more routines, and the fact that nothing much has happened in an average week leaves us thinking that the time has gone more quickly than it really has.

If that's so, about the only thing we can do to stop time

running away with us is fill the unforgiving minute with sixty seconds' worth of distance run. In other words, stop sitting around for half of the afternoon in the front of the telly watching rubbishy quiz shows, get up, get out, and do something worthwhile. Which reminds me: I really must finish sorting those old golf balls.

In the Bunker!

There's a technique that psychiatrists sometime use when trying to assess whether or not a patient is doolally. They call it 'stimulation of an associative pattern by a word'. You probably know it better as the word-association game.

One person says a word and the next person has to shout out the first word that comes to his or her mind. (The *I'm Sorry, I Haven't a Clue* teams know it as Word for Word, which in their case is a *dis*association game in which players may say any word as long as it has no connection with the previous one.)

Supposing I were to start with the word 'retirement', I'd bet good money that the next player would say 'golf'. Well, five bob anyway. It certainly rates high enough on the list of popular retirement hobbies to be worth a punt.

Like travel, painting, cooking and baking, singing in a choir, doing charity work, golf is for all ages, but it especially appeals to the elderly because you don't have to be very good to enjoy it; it's extremely sociable, involves an agreeable amount of elbow lifting and good-natured banter; it enables you to be competitive while not looking as if you are trying; and it's one of the few outdoor activities in which it is extremely difficult to injure yourself. Most importantly of all, you can go on playing it however decrepit you are, and if you've got to the stage when you find walking a bit of a trial, you can always swan round the course in a buggy.

There is a down side, which is that golf can be and often is one of the most infuriating games ever invented. P. G. Wodehouse – a keen golfer and one of the greatest writers about golf – understood that better than anyone.

Golf, he wrote in a short story entitled 'The Magic Plus Fours', 'acts as a corrective against sinful pride. I attribute the insane arrogance of the later Roman emperors almost entirely to the fact that, never having played golf, they never knew that strange chastening humility which is engendered by a topped chip shot. If Cleopatra had been ousted in the first round of the Ladies' Singles, we should have heard a lot less of her proud imperiousness.'

One of the great advantages of golf, especially for the elderly, is that there is an unwritten rule that whenever anything goes wrong, it is never your fault. This is particularly helpful for the older player for whom a lot of things can go wrong and usually do, and a round of golf can all too often turn out to be a long walk punctuated by eighteen disappointments.

Only a 19-handicap golfer can truly appreciate the Oldest Member's comments on the behaviour of young Mitchell Holmes in 'Ordeal by Golf', one of Wodehouse's short stories in his collection, *The Clicking of Cuthbert*. Holmes, it seemed, had a habit of losing his temper on the golf course. 'He seldom played a round without becoming piqued, peeved or, in many cases, chagrined ... The least thing upset him on the links. He missed short putts because of the uproar of the butterflies in the adjoining meadows.'

For the golfer, age brings neither wisdom nor understanding. He knows perfectly well that the likelihood of his becoming a better player is negligible, but that doesn't stop him believing that he might be the exception to the rule and beat the odds. Endlessly frustrated, he will go to extraordinary lengths to express his feelings without upsetting his opponents or his partners in a mid-week foursome.

A friend of mine, intrigued by the small crowd that had gathered at the window of the bar in his golf club, joined them in time to see an elderly golfer hurling his bagful of golf clubs into the middle of a small pond, which was a feature of the area next to the practice putting green. He then marched off in the direction of the car park. Very soon afterwards he returned, rolled up his trouser legs and waded into the middle of the pond. He reached down into the water, seized the bag, unzipped the pocket on the side, pulled out his car keys, hurled the bag back into the water and marched back to the car park.

For the elderly and retired, many of whom miss the drama of office life, golf poses questions that are guaranteed to bring out the best in the most downbeat of us. How, enquires the non-golfer, can a man who has faced many trials and tribulations in his long life be daunted – terrified, even – by the prospect of having to chip from a nasty lie across a deep bunker and onto the green on the other side?

'No pressure,' his partner calls out cheerfully. Determined to keep his head down, his swing slow and his eyes on the ball, he stabs at it, lifts his head, and tops the ball straight into the sand.

'No problem,' his partner says as he puts down his putter and reaches for his sand iron. 'It's only a game.'

Why, one asks oneself, do we who have arrived at an age when all we want is a quiet and easy life put ourselves through such unnecessary agonies? Answer: because it's fun.

Lady golfers of a certain age do not, on the whole, laugh as much as their male counterparts. They take the game altogether more seriously. I was flabbergasted the first time I played in a mixed foursome (for the uninitiated, that means two teams of two taking alternate shots, as opposed to a four ball which is four separate players playing as individuals and hitting every ball, and takes blooming hours) when I suggested to my partner – a normally mild-mannered, easygoing, fun-loving woman – that because our opponents had ended up barely two feet from the hole that we should give them the putt and halve the hole.

If I had suggested a spot of wife-swapping, she could not have more outraged.

'Give them the putt?' she squawked. 'Certainly not. You men may like to let each off the hook when the going gets tough, but we ladies are made of sterner stuff. We *never* give putts!'

A golfing friend of mine – a man of some substance, not to say distinction – was partnering me in a match against some ladies when he received the hair-dryer treatment from one of our opponents for daring to place the flag on the green when it came to our turn to putt.

'It's perfectly easy,' she said. 'The player who is not putting holds the flag in one hand. He does not drop it on the ground like a used sweet wrapper.'

'I've never been spoken to like that in my life,' he muttered out of the corner of his mouth as we stood there, as shame-faced as schoolboys caught cheating at conkers, watching the ladies putt.

Men on the whole, and especially the older ones, take their golf reasonably light-heartedly. They like to win, if they can, and they like to play as well as possible, but the last thing they want is to seem ungenerous and ungracious – in victory or in defeat.

Some golf clubs have a club within their club that caters for the older player. Ours is all-male and as doughty a bunch of senior citizens as you will find anywhere. We are called the Treacleminers (origins vary slightly depending on who you speak to) and we meet every Wednesday morning at nine when the head honcho decides who is going to play with whom and who against whom. It usually works out as planned, but there is often mild confusion as so-and-so hasn't turned up, or has forgotten, and nobody knows if he's coming or else somebody else has appeared who didn't say he was going to, so you can never be entirely sure that the person you thought you were about to partner and the pair you thought you were to compete against are the same people you will meet on the first tee, if at all.

But no one is surprised and no one really minds. The chances are you're going to have a good game, with like-minded people who have like-minded physical ailments, and with whom one can often have the most unexpected and absorbing conversations.

Younger players are sometimes rather diffident about bringing talk of their jobs and professions onto the golf course with
them, but men whose careers are long past are perfectly happy
to talk about the lives they have known, the people they have
met, and the experiences they have had.

I once played with a man who seemed quite a bit older than
me and was clearly less able-bodied, since he went round on
an electric scooter.

He was wearing shorts over unusually brown knees and I
asked him if by any chance he had lived abroad. Yes, he said, he
had hardly lived in England at all. After Korea, he had stayed in
the Far East and hadn't returned to England for years.

When he said Korea, did he mean he was in the Korean
War? Indeed he was, he said, and it was a matter of lasting
regret to him that so few people knew anything about it and
that it was so poorly memorialised.

I could barely remember it as a schoolboy, but certain
names and places featured strongly in my memory: the
Battle of the Imjin River, the Glorious Glosters and their CO,
Colonel Carne, VC, and big Bill Speakman, also the holder
of a Victoria Cross.

My golfing partner spoke of them and of others, and of the
cruel winter weather and the fact that for a year he and his
men never slept anywhere except out in the open – often in
temperatures of minus 20, never in a sleeping bag and always
with their boots on.

I have no idea who won that game, nor what the score was,
nor do I care. But the conversation I had with that Korean
veteran, walking alongside him on his electric scooter, will
remain with me for ever.

The really great thing about golf is that, unlike many amateur games, there is no obvious reason why one should ever stop playing. I sometimes walk the dog early in the morning on a nearby golf course when there is nobody about, but once a week I have to make a few detours because of three chaps who on that particular day, come rain, come shine, turn out and play nine holes together.

They are, respectively, eighty-three, eighty-five and eighty-nine.

Grandad Dancing

When I have fears, as Keats had fears,
Of the moment I'll cease to be . . .

The beginning of Noël Coward's touching poem about the thoughts that console him as he contemplates his exit stage right. Friends, in particular. I'm rather more concerned about the friends I might find myself having to take up with in the event of my bashing on far longer than I expect and all my old friends having 'gone on before', as the saying used to be – or 'passed' as people now say when they can't bring themselves to say 'died'.

One of my worries is that I might find myself at an old-age ballroom dancing class in the middle of the morning, trotting round a dusty church hall in the arms of a plump widow as we swoop up and down to the strains of Victor Silvester playing his signature tune, 'You're Dancing on My Heart'. Or, God forbid, on my feet.

On the plus side, it might give me the perfect opportunity to display some of my ballroom moves that were the talk of teenage Surrey in the mid-fifties.

Possibly the sole opportunity, since the only 'dancing' one seems to find oneself doing these days is jigging around vaguely in time with the music, hoping it will stop before you do.

One would love to be able to throw away one's inhibitions and dance like the young – dervishly, bouncing up and down, arms punching the air – but unfortunately all too many of us are hard put to raise our arms much above our chests, and so we just leave them dangling pathetically at our sides.

If you want one sure way of embarrassing your children, next time you are all invited to a wedding, take to the floor in a spirited, un-coordinated half-baked version of the twist.

Having been a talented exponent in the very early sixties, I recently made the mistake of trying to explain the dance to Tug.

I can't remember now how the subject came up. I think it was the occasion when I told her that I had never been to a club in London. The Garrick, the Beefsteak, Boodles, that kind of club, of course. But not what she and her friends would call a club. I had never been 'clubbing'.

'*Never?*' If I'd said I'd never heard of Beyoncé I could not have aroused a louder squawk of utter disbelief.

'That isn't to say I've never been into a night club,' I said. 'In my skiing days in the sixties I went to clubs in Swiss resorts with names like *Le Scotch* every night.'

'And did you dance in clubs like that?'

'Non-stop,' I said. 'Those were the great days of the Madison.'

'The what?'

'Have you ever seen a film called *Hairspray*?'

She shook her head.

'Well, if you do, you'll see them doing the Madison. It was

great. The best-ever line dance. Someone ought to bring it back. *It's Madison time. Hit it.*'

I demonstrated a few simple moves – two up, two back, followed by the big strong basketball with the Wilt Chamberlain hook.

'Are you serious?' she said.

'Sorry,' I said. 'I missed the hand clap.'

'Right,' she said. There was a pause. 'Was that the same thing as the twist?'

'No, no. The twist was late fifties, early sixties,' I said with all the seriousness of an academic on a Melvyn Bragg programme discussing the importance of *hamartia* in Greek tragedy, as described by Aristotle in his *Poetics*. 'Chubby Checker. "Let's Twist Again" and all that. It's what you see silly old fools doing at weddings. Trying to remember their glory days, and making a total mess of it.'

Of course, I should have seen it coming from a mile off, but when Tug said would I demonstrate it, she really meant it. Memories of my winning performance in the twist competition at the Brancaster Staithe Sailing Club dance in 1960 crowded in and the next thing I knew I was on my feet, wiggling everything in sight and out, and eventually pulling a muscle in my bottom.

'Mind you,' I said, lowering myself gingerly onto the sofa, 'that kind of free-style dancing wasn't around when I first started meeting girls. Teenage dances were the thing, and that meant you had to learn to dance different sorts of dances: the quickstep; the slow quickstep; the waltz, quick and slow. The Gay Gordons.'

'Friends of yours?' said Tug.

'Very funny.'

Before I knew what, I was on a nostalgic roll, explaining that I was just sixteen when I went to my first proper dance. It was during the Christmas holidays in 1955 and was given by Mr and Mrs Muspratt-Williams and Mr and Mrs Vange-Fobbing to celebrate their daughters' birthdays.

(Actually, I made those names up. I can't even begin to remember who gave the dance, for whom or for what. All I do know is that in those days dances were nearly always shared between two families.)

There was a small band called the Don Smith Trio (or was it the Ron Smith Trio?) comprising piano, drums and trumpet. It wasn't the Benny Goodman Orchestra exactly, but it did do a super version of 'Making Whoopee'. There was usually a kind of fruit cup thing to drink, which wasn't bad. Most of the girls were pretty boring, but some were quite jolly.

'The important thing,' I explained, 'was to get a really nice one lined up for the last waltz, because that's when they turned the lights down and you could dance cheek to cheek, which could be jolly good fun – especially if you had a partner who didn't mind being kissed.'

'Didn't *mind*?' squawked Tug. 'What does that mean, exactly? Didn't mind? Either you like someone and want to kiss them and them to kiss you, but no one kisses anyone because they don't *mind*.'

'You're quite right,' I said. 'Perhaps I should rephrase that ...'

'And, anyway, what's this thing about dancing cheek to cheek?' she wanted to know.

'It means exactly that,' I said, rather tersely. 'In my day you danced politely in the normal position unless, or until, you felt you knew your partner well enough to dance a bit closer, with the side of your face – i.e., your cheek – against theirs. It's what was known as dancing cheek to cheek, as in the Fred Astaire song.'

'Who?'

'Never mind.'

Tug said, 'If you fancy someone, the last thing you want to dance close to is their cheek.'

'What else would you dance close to? It was great.'

'Yuck,' she said. 'All hot and sweaty.'

'That was what was great about it. Some of my friends took it a lot less seriously than others. One chap I knew went to a dance with a Wall's pork sausage in his pocket. He was dancing cheek to cheek with a girl called Amanda. They had just finished their second snog when he pulled out the sausage and said, "Would you mind holding that for me?" Which she did, and had to be taken out and given a glass of water.'

'That's disgusting,' Tug said.

'No more disgusting than all that gyrating that passes for dancing these days.'

'You only say that because you can't do it. Like everyone else of your age.'

'May I remind you that you are speaking of—'

'I know. The man who won the twist competition at some yacht club.'

'Sailing club, actually.'

'Whatever.'

'Anyway, the point I'm trying to make is that in those days dancing was something you had to learn to do before you went to your first party. There was usually someone in the neighbourhood who gave dancing lessons on Saturday mornings. One of the girls who lived next door but one and I joined a class in the ballroom of the local hotel. We learnt the quickstep, the slow quickstep, the waltz and the Viennese waltz, which is the quick one. Usually to a record of Victor Silvester and his Orchestra. Strict tempo stuff, given a light touch by Oscar Grasso on the lead violin. The woman who taught us owned a large white poodle and she would demonstrate the steps with the poodle standing on its hind legs.

'Too much information,' she said. 'And actually quite obscene.'

'Eccentric, certainly. Also it's very difficult to dance cheek to cheek with a dog.'

'How would you know? Don't say you had to dance with the poodle as well.'

'Don't be silly.'

'Who's calling who silly?' she said.

Is it my imagination, or did I treat my grandfather (the only one I knew) with deep respect, verging on awe? The idea that I might have suggested, to his face, that he was being silly, is unimaginable. But then what isn't for a modern teenager listening to a grandfather rambling up and down memory lane?

Could Tug really believe that for a sixteen-year-old boy, at home for the holidays from boarding school, the prospect of his first close encounter with a girl was as unnerving as it was exciting?

I had always been a timorous child. While my friend from down the road, Nigel, threw himself into every new adventure that came his way and somehow, even when things turned out badly, always seemed to come away having enjoyed himself, I invariably approached everything fearing the worst.

Those were the days when parents – my mother in particular – didn't believe in bolstering their children's confidence, and if ever they exhibited the slightest sign of showing off they were slapped down very quickly indeed.

The memory of the moments leading up to my first dance remain ineradicably etched on my mind, and may well be one of those episodes that psychiatrists seize on when trying to fathom some deep psychological flaw.

I remember coming down the stairs feeling quite chipper, dressed rather self-consciously in my father's dinner jacket. It fitted, as my mother would have said, where it touched, and had a light green tinge to it here and there, not to say a faint smell of mothballs. My father's attempts to tie his single-ended bow tie from behind me had ended not in disaster but definite disappointment. Suffice to say it drooped.

So did my hair. Standing in front of the mirror in the hall, I tried one more time to straighten my sad tie, but rather than risk it coming undone altogether, gave it up as a bad job. Anyway, it didn't look that bad. With the help of a dab of my father's hair cream, I had managed to smarm my hair against my scalp in the hope that I looked a bit like Denis Compton. Unfortunately, there was this annoying tuft at the back which kept popping up and I was trying to flatten it with the palms of my hands when my mother came in from the kitchen carrying supper on a tray. (A friend's father was taking us; my father was doing the collecting at midnight.) She glanced at my reflection in the mirror as she passed.

'I don't know why you're going to all this trouble,' she said. 'No one's going to look at you.'

'No way!' shouted Tug.

If I'd announced I been chosen to join the European Space Programme, she could not have goggled more.

For me, as a child of the forties and early fifties, parental put-downs were par for the course. Small wonder things started going downhill a bit from that moment on. I didn't get a partner in the Paul Jones; my tie came apart completely during the Gay Gordons; and the fruit cup ran out before I got there.

I managed to bag a girl just as the lights were going down and the band struck up the last waltz, but not, unfortunately, the one I'd had my eye on most of the evening, who was dancing cheek to cheek with a cocky boy from Hurst Green and, as far as I could make out in the semi-darkness, was kissing him. Emboldened by his devil-may-care behaviour, I asked my partner if it would be all right if I danced a bit closer to her.

'I'd rather you didn't,' she said. 'You've got a funny smell.'

So my mother was right, as usual. No one looked at me: not at close quarters, anyway. I wondered sometimes in those days if anyone ever would.

'And did they, Grandpa?' said Tug.

'They certainly did when I won the twist competition at the Brancaster Staithe Sailing Club dance.'

Freedom Pass

Seven years ago, on the occasion of his sixtieth birthday, Matthew Parris wrote a piece in *The Times* about the Freedom Pass to which he had just become entitled.

It seemed that he was embarrassed at the fact that he was suddenly able to travel free of charge on all types of public transport in London while surrounded by passengers who, clearly younger than him and probably less well off, were being asked to pay the full going rate for a ticket.

On the basis that Alan Coren and I had once done a programme for BBC Radio 4 called *Freedom Pass* in which, with the help of our passes, we had travelled hither and thither, mainly on buses, nattering together about more or less anything that came into our heads, I had a telephone call from the Radio 4 *PM* programme asking me if I would come in and discuss Matthew's problem with him on the show.

I began by suggesting that what he was really worried about was not the other passengers and any feelings of guilt they might have aroused in his sensitive soul, but the fact that he had hit sixty.

I said that the shock on realising that one had suddenly become a senior citizen was quite understandable; we had all experienced it. However, it was something that he would very soon get over, and after a while would be happily travelling around for free, like thousands of other sixty-somethings, and thinking nothing of it. More than that, he'd be reckoning he couldn't believe his luck and pouring blessings on the head of Transport for London – whoever he may be.

The conversation was friendly and amusing, though Matthew stuck to his guns, so I felt compelled to introduce some stronger arguments – the main one of which was that he, like me and countless others, had spent enough on travel in London during our lives that we could almost have bought our own Tube train, and that we jolly well deserved to be rewarded for decades of loyal service by the powers that be at TfL.

At that moment there came into my head, I know not how, a quotation from Shakespeare in which the Bard encapsulated all that I was trying to say, which he invariably does.

'You may remember the words of Othello,' I heard myself murmuring into the microphone in front of me, 'when he is told by Lodovico that he is to be arrested for seeming to have employed Iago to murder Cassio: "Soft you, a word or two before you go. I have done the state some service and they know't."'

Before Matthew had a chance to respond, we were told we were out of time and the conversation was brought an abrupt halt.

Friends who happened to hear the programme were seriously impressed by what seemed like a killer blow on my part – though, truth to tell, I completely sympathised with

Matthew's feelings, as would Alan have done, had he still been with us.

I distinctly remember a conversation we had when he and I reached sixty and he discovered he did not have to pay for his prescription to be dispensed; and, rather than admit he had hit the big six-oh, paid for his pills for many months before finally becoming reconciled to the status quo.

I, too, suffered some misgivings when I was first called upon to present my Freedom Pass to an inspector on a 19 bus, but very soon began to appreciate the value of being able to hop on and off any bus or Tube train of my choosing and travel the length and breadth of the capital without once having to put my hand in my pocket.

What's more, when buying a railway ticket to Norwich, say, or Basingstoke, one is not obliged to pay for any part of the journey included within the Freedom Pass area, and if one is also armed with a Senior Railcard, one gets a third off one's fare on top.

And having reached one's station, in the event of there being a local bus to take one on to one's destination, one simply pulls out one's Freedom Pass and on one rolls, at no personal expense or inconvenience. After half-past nine, that is.

Of all the threats that the Exchequer dream up in another desperate attempt to pay for the National Health, or benefits, or high-speed trains or whatever, the one that chills the blood of pensioners more quickly and more surely than any other is the suggestion that oldies who can afford it should pay their own bus and Tube fares like everyone else.

I can't help thinking that, after seven years of Freedom

Passing, Matthew Parris might not be as enthusiastic a supporter of such a move as he once was.

More to the point, who is to decide who can and who can't afford to cough up three quid to travel up the road to collect his or her prescription and back again?

And, anyway, it isn't the fact of having to shell out for even the shortest journey that would drastically change some people's lives, but the possibility of realising that one has got on to the wrong bus and the sooner one gets on to the right one the better.

Mapping one's way round the capital above and below ground is one of the greatest pleasures available to OAPs with time on their hands. If required to pay for this simple privilege, many would choose to stay at home and never go anywhere.

This is not meant as a party political broadcast on behalf of the aged, but as a celebration of one of the great benefits of old age, along, of course, with free medicine and free eye tests.

But hand-outs are not the only reason to feel that, with luck and good health, we late-middle-agers have plenty to look forward to.

At the stage I have reached, thoughts of living in a retirement home are some way from my mind, if not far. And yet the chances of spending one's final years in one's own home are, in the huge majority of cases, slim, verging on the non-existent. And, since my experience of such places has nearly all been as one visiting the sick, the frail and the batty, the prospect of being one of them is, if considered at all, somewhat daunting.

But then I turned once again to Diana Athill in her little

room, surrounded by a few loved possessions, and, in neighbouring rooms, her congenial friends.

The place she lives in in North London, run by the Mary Feilding Guild, who specialise in homes for the active and independent elderly, may be a shining exception in the retirement home world, yet the things that make her life happy are by no means exclusive to her and her fellow residents.

One is being able to live in a room that she has made her own – something my mother was able to do in her retirement home in Tobermory as it happened; another is being cared for by staff who are kind, thoughtful and respectful; the third is not having to worry about the sort of day-to-day problems that take up so much time and effort in the outside world.

As Miss Athill said, when the hot water went off one morning, her first thought was, Oh God, I must find a plumber, followed by a feeling of enormous relief when she remembered that it was not her responsibility. Somebody else would see to it. And somebody did. Straight away.

If she feels like going out shopping for a few bits and bobs, she can. If she doesn't feel up to it, there is always someone on hand who is only too happy to oblige.

She has written much about her love life, but, by her own admission, she realised at seventy-five that she was no longer 'a sexual being'. There are others, however, who have no plans for retirement of *any* sort. Only recently I heard a story of a retirement home whose staff were thrown into a complete tizzy when an aged male resident was found not only in the room of an aged female, but in her bed – where it appeared he had been for most of the previous night.

The lady in question was completely baffled by all the

hoo-ha that arose and reprimanded the manager by pointing out in no uncertain terms that not only did she not object to having a man in her bed, but that she had enjoyed it every bit as much as he had.

'Now that's what I call a Freedom Pass,' she said.

Ooty for Me

A few years ago, some friends of more or less our age – in their sixties, anyway – decided to pack up everything in England and move to the south of France.

They had been going there on holiday for years, sometimes several times a year. They had decided they liked it so much that they bought a really nice house in a little village up in the hills, with great views across the Provençal countryside, great food shops, great local restaurants and all that – in easy striking distance of Nice and Antibes.

Their chums came out to visit them. They took them to the Colombe d'Or in Saint Paul de Vence and the Chèvre d'Or in Eze, and they had outings to places of interest such as the Matisse Chapelle du Rosaire in Vence and Cocteau's Chapelle de Saint Pierre in Villefranche and the Villa Ephrussi de Rothschild on Cap Ferrat. And the chums lay in the sun round the pool, sipping pale rosé de Provence, and said, 'This is the life. You never know, we might end up as your neighbours.'

Occasionally they would return to England to see their children and grandchildren, and do a bit of shopping and see their friends, and it was to one of those that the wife revealed, quite out of the blue in response to a question about their life in a foreign country, 'Everything about France is wonderful. The food's wonderful. The wine's wonderful. The weather's wonderful. The only downside is the French.'

She paused. 'Oh,' she said, 'and the banks won't allow you to have an overdraft if you are not French.'

It seems a far cry from the days when ex-advertising man Peter Mayle bought a house in southern France in the late eighties and wrote a book about it called *A Year in Provence*, which became an international bestseller and was responsible for some of the thousands who subsequently followed his example. In buying a house, I mean, not writing an international bestseller.

Fortunately, the ones who have plumped for the other two favourite retirement homes for the Brits – Spain and Italy – would seem to be rather more welcome, though that doesn't stop them complaining. Speaking to an Englishman who owns two villas in Tuscany, one of which he lets out by way of supplementing his pension, one had the impression that it was not as straightforward as it sounded and that all sorts of 'pressures' from different quarters, official and unofficial (no names, no pack drill) could make life very difficult for him if they so chose.

One can put up with people who have, for one reason or another, decided to abandon the home of their birth and settle in a country where they neither speak the language, understand the culture or much like the food; but what gets up one's nose in no uncertain terms is the fact that so many of them take every opportunity to slag off the country they have left behind. More often than not, they do this when back here visiting family and friends.

Many of these southern European countries are home to old hands who can't remember when they lived anywhere else but abroad. Some left England for very particular reasons. It is no secret, for example, that one reason Somerset Maugham moved to France and spent the rest of his life in the Villa Mauresque on Cap Ferrat was that his private life was less than agreeable to his elder brother, who was a prominent High Court judge and later Lord Chief Justice.

Maugham was one of the richest men in the world, though his life of ease in a beautiful house in the South of France did not appear to make him very happy.

A friend of mine told me that his father once met the great man out there and thought to interest him by announcing, 'I, too, am an author.' 'And what have you written?' Maugham enquired. 'Two books on spear-fishing.' 'Indeed,' muttered Maugham and sidled away.

He was, by all accounts, at his happiest when east of Suez, and after watching two series of *The Real Marigold Hotel* on television, one can see why.

Leaving aside the fact that this had no connection with *The Best Exotic Marigold Hotel*, and that movie itself bore little resemblance to Deborah Moggach's witty novel, *These Foolish Things*, on which it was loosely based, beyond the fact that they were both about English OAPs in search of a warm, congenial, comfortable and affordable retirement in India, the BBC's version of the story using aged celebs bore even less.

In the first series Miriam Margolyes, Wayne Sleep, Sylvester McCoy and Jan Leeming, among others, were flown to Jaipur, where they stayed in a very nice little hotel and were gently introduced to the Indian way of life and gradually (though rather more gradually than the rest in the case of Miss Margolyes, who was in a perpetual state of anxiety over her lavatory requirements) got to understand something about it and to like it, to the extent that by the end they mostly agreed that it might even be possible for people of their age to retire there.

Series two featured a similar mixture of vaguely famous faces in the shapes of erstwhile Three Degrees singer Sheila Ferguson, Dr Miriam Stoppard, World Snooker champion Dennis Taylor, naturalist and ex-Goodie Bill Oddie, actor Paul Nicholas, chef Rustie Lee, *Carry On* actress Amanda Barrie and ... no-o-o-o ... yes! Lionel Blair: eighty-two and still dancing.

Just like the first lot, their initial reaction to Kochi on the south-west coast of India, where they were to spend a month, was sceptical, though by the last episode they were all mad about the place and the people and the strange customs and the alternative treatments for their assorted ailments, and the feeling of calm that had descended over them. Which was amazing, given the number of events they attended, including a tigerfest, during which we were afforded the astonishing sight of a bare-chested Bill Oddie painted in tiger stripes, his nipples as orange as a pair of Belisha beacons.

Later, he, Dennis, Paul, Miriam and Rustie were taken on a wildlife trip among the tea plantations at Parkside, high in the Nilgiri mountains, with views to the horizon on all sides.

'It's like Shangri-La,' Miriam murmured.

This was part of a stay in Ooty, a town built by the British army in the nineteenth century as a retreat from the worst heat of an Indian summer, the temperature up there being the closest to that of Britain in all of the subcontinent.

It was here, in the wonderfully old-fashioned Ooty Club, that Dennis did something that he could never have dreamed of as a budding young snooker player: he played the game on the very table on which it was invented by an English officer called Neville Chamberlain. No relation.

Later they were shown retirement flats costing a mere twenty-five grand, and met a couple of female residents. They looked rather too young for such a place, but, as they pointed out, everyone does everything much earlier in India than in England.

'The climate's perfect,' said Dennis. 'There's no humidity; no mosquitoes. It's Ooty for me all the time.'

'We're all in love with India,' Miriam declared when they all met up later, and so said all of them in various ways and in various places.

'I would truly wish that every single person should come to India,' said Bill Oddie, for whom perhaps the biggest surprise was not the Indians but his fellow explorers. 'People of this age can be bloody witty,' he said.

'This,' said Amanda, 'is the retirement home we've all been looking for, and we've found it. Look how happy we've all been.'

Was it any wonder? They'd all had a whale of a time, but did any of it bear any relation to the sort of life they might lead were they to decide to spend their old age there? How could they tell? How could we? This was a television programme: an entertainment for the viewers, a junket for the celebs. It was as much a PR exercise (on behalf of the owners of chic retirement apartments and old people's homes as any that I experienced as a travel writer in the eighties), and for a month they had lived, as Amanda said, 'in a little bubble'. A bubble, one felt, that were one to take the plunge and move there, might all too easily burst.

Programmes like *The Real Marigold Hotel* are hugely appealing to anyone planning their retirement. As Paul Nicholas, the philosopher-in-chief of the group, said, 'You cannot sit and look at the telly all day long, saying "I'm seventy-plus." You have to keep mobile when you're older, and you've got to be interested, because just to be sedentary and not take part in life, it's a downward spiral into real old age.'

I doubt there are many among us who have not at some time or other toyed, however briefly, with the idea of upping sticks and heading for warmer and cheaper climes. Though perhaps not to somewhere as unfamiliar as India. The culture shock might be enough to bump some people off within hours of getting there.

Had Lionel and Sheila and Bill and the others not been cossetted and kept busy and interested, and been introduced to warm, welcoming locals who gave them lovely things to do and threw jolly parties for them, there's no knowing how soon one or two of them might have decided India was not for them and been on the phone to the PR people booking their passage back to Blighty.

For those of our age who were born and brought up in India before partition, it is still their home, and when they go back there, they feel they are back *chez eux* again. But few stayed on, and just as few think of going back there to live.

Their lives are here – perhaps with a little *gîte* in France or a farmhouse in Tuscany which they visit whenever they want. That is all the expatriate life they could wish for now.

Even as I write, the BBC and the creators of *The Real Marigold Hotel* are launching a series called *Second Chance Summer: Tuscany*, in which ten total strangers, mostly in their fifties and united only by a wish to change their lives, spend two months on a fifty-acre estate, including a vineyard and olive trees, seeing if they can run it.

Will they succeed? Will there be terrible rows, and personality clashes, and moments of revelation? Will they fulfil their dreams? Who knows. Who cares? It's showbiz. Anyway, *Marigold* No. 3 should be along any minute now.

Tell-Tale Signs

Having established early on in this book that I am still enjoying the pleasures of late middle age, and having aired a few random thoughts about the prospect of senectitude and tossed out a few examples based on the experiences of others who are that little bit older than me, I feel I still haven't fully established to my satisfaction – and therefore perhaps to any readers who might have picked it up – what being old really means.

Neither, I'm glad to say, have most of my friends. A couple, both comfortably into their seventies, arrived recently at St Pancras Station after holidaying in France and were having quite a time of it, what with getting off the train with their suitcases, staggering through the milling crowds towards the exit, shuffling along in the taxi queue. Having heaved themselves aboard and slumped into their seats, the wife said to the husband, 'God, that was hard work.' 'Very,' said the husband. 'Can you imagine what it's going to be like when we're old?'

How *do* people know when they're old? Some clues are

obvious. Try dropping the name Profumo into a conversation, or mention Manfred Mann or the Sex Pistols, and if you get a blank look you can start fearing the worst.

Speaking to one's own generation, or better still the generation ahead, is generally more reassuring. A doughty woman friend of mine, whom I have partnered on the golf course from time to time, once remarked that she didn't really feel old until she was eighty. Well, she is now nearly ninety and it was only last year that she gave up driving – and she still plays golf. And, at the time of writing, the great Nicholas Parsons is still chairing *Just a Minute* at ninety-four.

I think that, at that sort of age, one could reasonably claim to be old. The years cannot be denied. And yet one need only be in one's sixties to be referred to as 'elderly', a 'senior citizen', or even 'veteran'.

At sixty, one qualifies for all sorts of hand-outs – Freedom Pass, Senior Railcard, free sight tests, free medicine, state pension, you name it; and you might suppose from that that sixty is, officially speaking, old.

Yet, from the little research I have done on the subject, online and among friends, I have come across many different definitions, such as 'the end of the human life cycle', 'the last period of life', 'being retired', and have come to the conclusion that no one can say for certain when old age begins.

I read an article somewhere which put the blame for all this confusion on the Baby Boomers who, wishing to put paid to old age, invented things like Viagra and cosmetic surgery and Spanx leggings so that they could all seem far younger than they really are.

Such conclusion as they were able to reach suggested that

the definition of old age depends on who you happen to be speaking to at the time.

For a thirteen-year-old it would be thirty, for a thirty-year-old it would be fifty, and for a fifty-year-old it would be seventy-something. Beyond that, you're probably wise not to ask.

All this was based on some survey or other. But then I have read about a survey of two thousand people over forty by something called the Sunrise Blog, which revealed that most of them believe old age starts at eighty.

My theory is that something will happen, or you'll notice something, or someone will point something out, which will set the alarm bells ringing and you'll know at that moment that, as my tutor at Oxford said to me after I got a third-class degree, it's a straight run to the grave.

Here, then, is my own personal checklist of tell-tale signs:

The Dyson Airblade hand dryer

Next time you wash your hands in a motorway service station, or a gourmet restaurant, or a theatre loo, and you plunge your hands between the blades of Sir James Dyson's brilliant invention, quickly check to see if the skin on the back of them is puckering like the neck of a marine iguana. If so, you have not been magically transported to the land of the living dead, but you are a lot older than you realised. And if the sight freaks you out, remember next time to use a towel dispenser, or wipe your hands on your trouser legs/shirt front/whatever, and get over it.

The little old lady on the pavement

The kindest gestures can sometimes backfire. Once, on a particularly cold day in London when the snow on the pavements had turned to ice, I spotted a little old lady standing hesitantly beside a busy road as the traffic roared past in both directions. I offered my arm, which she gratefully took, and as we set off together I slipped and fell flat on my back. Luckily she turned out to be an expert in first aid and couldn't have been kinder or more helpful. I told my friend the story and confessed that I felt like a silly old fool. 'Old?' he said. 'You think *you're* old? The last little old lady I helped across a street was my wife.'

The phantom raspberry-blower of Old London Town

Not for nothing are senior citizens referred to as old farts. Healthy walks with chums are often enlivened by what sound like a series of tiny grunts. Sometimes these are exactly what they are. Suffering from aches and pains, as the elderly inevitably do, the involuntary 'oof' sound becomes an integral part of their subconscious vocabulary. But in the event of their having eaten rather too many Brussels sprouts, or having overdone it with the Camembert, the need to relieve the pressure becomes overwhelming.

Naturally one doesn't wish to emulate the explosive and murderous skills of the Victorian petomaniac in Ronnie Barker's classic sketches, but all too often one has little say in the matter, and one can only hope that superhuman self-control will result in a socially acceptable outcome.

That, of course, depends on how good one's companions' hearing is, not to say one's own. A lot of old people could barely hear a thunderstorm if it was slap over their heads, so they assume that if they can't hear themselves letting one go, neither can anyone else – especially if they stagger the emissions, so to speak. This does not, on the whole, help.

The older one gets, the greater the chances that one doesn't even know one has done anything, and you will sometimes find old people toddling along with smiles on their face, farting gently in time to their steps.

Times twelve and a half over a hundred

I was never any good at maths at school – to wit, the 4 per cent I got in my entrance exam when I was twelve. And I'm guessing I only did as well as that because I spelt my name correctly at the top of the page. So I never got to experience the thrill of higher maths, I have never discovered what Hilbert's twenty-four problems are, and as for any clever clogs hoping to win the million-dollar prize for solving the Yang-Mills Existence and Mass Gap, let me reassure him or her that I am no threat.

Nevertheless, for all my feeble attempts to master quadratic equations or to remember that in right-angled triangles the square of the hypotenuse is equal to the sum of the square of the other two sides, I was – or so I imagined – sufficiently equipped to do such basic things as add, subtract, multiply and divide simple amounts. I was also, when young, reasonably handy at mental arithmetic. So when I got to the age when I started taking girls out to dinner, I was quite capable of working out the tip without having to resort to paper and pencil.

Can I do it now? Can anyone of my age? Apparently not. Next time you see a man in a restaurant staring at a bill and trying to add up on his fingers, you'll know you're looking at a typical picture of old age.

Like pistol shots

Time was when I took pride in the way I tended my toenails. I doubt the country's best podiatrist could have held a candle to my artistry. These days, I am about as much use in the toe department as a chocolate teapot. And I am not the only one of my age who feels the same way. As one gets older, one's nails become so thick and hard that a normal pair of nail scissors can't make the faintest impression on them, let alone cut them. Professional chiropodists' clippers are required, but they're a fat lot of use if you're so stiff in the back that, however hard you try to bend down you can't get within a fourpenny bus ride of them.

Help is called for, though rarely given with good grace. I remember a friend describing how, every time he went to see his elderly father, he was asked to 'have a go at the piggies'. He once described cutting the paternal toenails as 'like a series of pistol shots'.

Organ Recital

'Ten minutes and not a second more.' That, generally speaking, is the rule adopted by old friends when meeting for lunch or a drink, regarding the amount of time they allow themselves for swapping tales of their latest aches, pains and afflictions before getting down to the serious business of eating and drinking.

Hardly a day goes by when I don't hear of another friend who has had to have a new hip or a new knee or a new head or something. Add to those the pacemaker insertions, the aortic valve replacements, the heart bypasses, the prostate removals, the rotator cuff repairs, the Dupuytren's contractures and the cataract surgery, and I find myself wondering if there is anyone I know who can still boast any of the bits and pieces he was born with.

Is it any wonder that, as we are all beginning to discover as the years pile up, ten minutes is scarcely enough to scratch the surface of one's latest medical condition?

Only yesterday I bumped into an old friend, who said he'd come from chairing an important debate. I couldn't tell you what the subject was because within seconds we were swapping our medical histories, and having given him a brief, though detailed, account of my long-running back problem, followed by the latest on Mrs Matthew's cataract operation, we barely had time to draw breath before he was regaling us with something to do with something or other that isn't quite right and may need investigating.

From what we could gather, a colonoscopy was on the menu, and when you get to our age you know how unappealing that can be – even if you have never undergone one yourself.

For the uninitiated, it's the method whereby a doctor can examine the inner lining of your large intestine, using a flexible tube, to see if you have any ulcers or polyps, or excessive bleeding. In layman terms, it's a camera up your bottom, and very uncomfortable it is too. Or so one gathers from those who have experienced it.

It's also quite embarrassing. Speaking as one who was brought up to believe that one's body is a sacred temple – or at the very least a private place, open only to the owner and a few very close friends and only by invitation – the idea of having its most intimate secrets explored by a comparative stranger and his associates is akin to a serious invasion of privacy, even if those leading the charge are wearing white coats and rubber gloves.

However, there comes a moment in all our lives (unless we happen to be bionic) when things begin to fall apart and it's not just the centre that cannot hold.

For obvious reasons I do not feel qualified to discuss the sort of medical problems that women encounter in the later stages of their lives (in fact, I'm not entirely sure what they are), but when it comes to us blokes, they usually boil down to heart, prostate, hip/knee replacement and pills for conditions for which they have been prescribed but can't now remember what.

As things stand – or more to the point, as *I* stand – my knees would appear to holding up pretty well for my age. This is immensely reassuring, since by coincidence I recently met a man at a dinner party who turned out to be an orthopaedic surgeon specialising in knees. Naturally, I seized the opportunity for a brief – and free – consultation.

'If anyone comes to see me with a dodgy knee,' he said, tactfully deploying a decidedly informal, hail-fellow-well-met manner, 'and they ask me if they should have their knee replaced, I tell them three things. One, it will be very painful. Two, it will take quite a long time to recover. Three, the knee you have now is the best knee you will ever have.'

Not much help for anyone who can hardly get out of a chair, I'm sure you'll agree, but I've no doubt he will have caused many a potential patient suffering from the odd mild tweak to have second thoughts.

A dicky heart can also be a problem for anyone who is no longer young at it. I had mine checked not too long ago and was told that I had the heart of a sixteen-year-old.

'As long as you haven't got the brain to go with it,' said Tug when I happened to mention it.

'I'll pretend I didn't hear that,' I said.

So, that just leaves the prostate. No problem there. Personally speaking, I don't have one any more. I discovered I had a tumour in it sixteen years ago and had the whole thing removed.

The operation in those days was a lot more aggressive than it is now. Indeed, my first words in the recovery room were, 'I knew this was going to be invasive, but I didn't imagine I was going to wake up feeling like Poland.'

As I recall, it did not get me the chuckle I had been hoping for.

Doctors, I have decided, only like jokes when they're the ones telling them.

The best jokes, of course, are the ones that aren't jokes at all. They're real stories about real people. Like the elderly, somewhat old-fashioned friend of mine – a man of distinction and success, blessed with a delightful ignorance of the modern world – who was lying on his side on the couch in a GP's surgery, being examined for possible symptoms of this and that, and suddenly, to his astonishment, realised that the doctor had inserted his finger into his bottom.

Describing the incident later, in brief outline rather than detail, he concluded, in the solemn tones of a bishop in a pulpit, 'All I can say is that I am very glad I'm not a homosexual.'

A Bite on the Bum

Many years ago I was sitting in our drawing room in London, being interviewed by some journalist or other about a book of mine that had just been published, when the burglar alarm went off.

This came as something of a surprise, since it was eleven o'clock in the morning, the alarm had long since been turned off, and there was no way it could turn itself on. Somebody elsewhere in the house must have interfered with it by accident.

The person responsible turned out to be our cleaning lady, who had been dusting in the hall where the alarm controls were. Apart from the little panel where you put in the code, there was a small box with a square red button on the top which was to be pushed down only in the event of an emergency. Once activated, a message automatically went through to the police station and cancellation was impossible.

We discovered all that later. What happened a few minutes after the alarm went off was that two police cars came screaming down the road, sirens blaring, pulled up outside our house, and four policemen were on our doorstep, demanding entry. I have a feeling that a couple of fire engines may have turned up as well.

The policemen tore round the house, up and down stairs, in and out of every room, checking that we were not being burgled, or held as hostages by some mad group, or having heart attacks.

It was quite a show. The two of us sat there quietly throughout, and when they had all gone I was able to apologise and explain the reason for this dramatic interruption.

'Oh,' said the journo. 'I thought you did it to make yourself seem more interesting.'

Time was when I was up for any form of publicity, and though I never went quite so far as to create a real-life drama purely for the purposes of flogging a book, I would have gone to considerable lengths to come up with something that might catch potential readers' attention, if not interest.

These days, as old age tiptoes ever closer, the idea that anything that has happened in my life might be of the remotest interest to anyone is absurd. And yet, writing about the prospect of old age and thinking back over the last seventy-plus years, I realise that, unwittingly, I have been polishing up certain events in a way that suggests my life has not been thoroughly humdrum from soup to nuts.

I make no apology for this. Which of us has not at some time in our lives been susceptible to a touch of Munchausenish invention?

Exaggeration is not a sin. It can hardly be called lying. It is not as deliberate as that, although it may begin with an urge to impress and thereby make oneself seem more interesting.

Many have fallen prey to this temptation and have been found out. During her 2008 presidential campaign Hillary Clinton described how, a dozen years earlier, she had landed in Bosnia under heavy sniper fire, yet a video recording clearly showed her strolling with her daughter towards a crowd of local children and being hugged by them.

People are, on the whole, polite when listening to other people's stories; they are disinclined to challenge them. As a result, the tall story gets repeated and eventually takes the place of the real one.

I am as guilty of exaggeration as anyone, and one drama in particular has become something of a staple whenever the subject of my health crops up – which is not unusual – and relates to my bad back.

Almost everyone of my age seems to have one. A dodgy back, that is. In some cases, the causes are serious and the results catastrophic, and many's the time I have had the pros and cons of back surgery described to me in such detail that I have come to realise that my own problems are as insignificant as a head cold compared with double pneumonia.

The general opinion among the doctors, physiotherapists, internet advisers and so on whom I have consulted on the subject is that the sort of back pain I have is down to decrepitude and is commonly found in people over seventy. In short, I have osteoarthritis – a degenerative joint disease that usually occurs with age and of which the symptoms generally include joint pain and stiffness.

How boring is that? 'Usually', 'generally', 'commonly' ... so run-of-the mill it's hardly worth mentioning.

Or is it? I think it is generally agreed that any injuries one might have sustained in one's life, however well treated and overcome, have a habit of coming back and, as one doctor put it, 'biting you on the bum'.

I heard myself telling an ex-army officer the other day that a riding accident when I was twelve had put paid to my chances of a military career, and that it was a source of constant regret to me that I had not been able to serve my country – thereby implying in one sentence a) that I was out hunting at the time with the Quorn, if not riding in the Grand National, and b) that it had been my childhood dream to serve my country.

Perhaps Dr Johnson was right on the money when he declared that 'Every man thinks meanly of himself for not having been a soldier', but I have to admit that I don't feel quite as badly about it as the old pub bore suggested.

But being turned down for National Service because you have failed the medical is not quite the same as having your chosen career snatched from you through no fault of your own. I daresay I would have made the best of it, had I been accepted and – who knows – been commissioned into one of the Guards regiments and become a debs' delight, but, actually, it came as a great relief to be told I was medically Grade 4 and that I wouldn't have to waste two years of my life before going to university, which I might very well have done since National Service had pretty well ground to a halt.

I suspect that I was trying to make myself sound more interesting – to myself, mainly. It certainly failed as far as my army friend was concerned. He muttered something to the effect that he himself had been in the Guards and enquired if he could buy me a drink.

I really did once sustain a riding injury, and I have always thought it has a lot to answer for, but for a different and much more obvious reason: namely this dodgy back which has dogged me for years and has recently returned in no uncertain terms – though actually it was describing the boy iPhoning from horseback in Hyde Park to the grandchildren that reminded me and sent me trotting off down memory lane.

'It must be quite difficult to fall off a horse when it's just walking,' Tug had said.

'It could suddenly throw you off,' I'd suggested, 'and in my case one did.'

'One did what?'

'Threw me off.'

'While it was walking?'

'Galloping, actually.'

'Cool. When did this happen?'

'1962. On Hosey Common, just up the hill from Westerham in Kent. Not far from where Winston Churchill lived. Rather appropriate, really.'

'Why? Did he fall off his horse?' Ludo enquired.

'Not as far as we know. He was a cavalry officer in his youth: commissioned into the 4th Hussars before joining an attachment of the 21st Lancers and taking part in one of the last great cavalry charges in history at the Battle of Omdurman. I doubt he went to the sort of riding school I did.'

'You went to a riding school?' said Ludo.

'Everyone I knew did in those days. Parents brought their children up to be equipped with a modicum of social skills: riding, dancing, tennis, bridge, that sort of thing.'

'I didn't know you could play bridge,' said Tug.

'I can't,' I said. 'It was just an example.'

'But you were taught to ride.'

'I was taught the rudiments. How to get on.'

'How to fall off?' said Ludo.

'Har, har. The most important thing is to learn how to sit.'

'You mean apart from lowering your bottom?'

'A horse isn't some kind of armchair,' I said. 'There's a way of sitting properly on a horse: back straight, elbows in, ball of foot on tread of stirrup, toes pointing slightly upwards.'

Of course they then wanted to know where this riding school was.

I explained that I went to two. The first one, when I was about nine, was at a place called Crockham Hill, where I used to go by bus (on my own) every Saturday morning. The owner of the stables was Miss Rogers. Mention her name to anyone who learnt to ride with her and the blood runs cold in their veins.

She was a small woman, slightly bent and brown and wizened, and seemed to all of us to be older than God. She was what used to be called a martinet.*

In addition to insisting that we maintained an upright posture in the saddle with our hands on the reins at stomach level and the stirrups beneath the balls of our feet, we had to saddle and bridle our ponies before setting out, remove them on our return and rub their coats down before we were allowed to catch the bus home.

---

* Noun: a person who demands complete obedience; a strict disciplinarian. Originally a scourge-like whip with about ten leather lashes, applied to the calves or bare buttocks, especially in France and other European countries. Can also be used as an implement in erotic spanking – though not in Miss Rogers's case.

Anyone deviating in any way from the rules of riding, as taught by Miss Rogers, would not only have felt the rough side of her tongue, but might easily have been made to stay behind and clean out the stables – a labour that even Hercules might have baulked at.

'Did you learn how to jump and everything?' said Ludo.

'Not everything, but I could trot elegantly, and I had a nice seat.'

'I thought it was called a saddle.'

'Do you want to hear about my accident or not?' I said.

Tug said, 'Is there going to be blood? If there's going to be blood, I might faint.'

'I won't,' said Ludo.

I never fell off at Miss Rogers's, but when I went away to prep school we had riding lessons with a man in Westerham who was nothing like as responsible. I mean, none of us wore riding hats or anything like that.

January 1952 was especially cold. The ground was frozen and riding was cancelled for a couple of weeks, so by the time we all went out next, the horses were in a particularly frisky mood. I was stuck on a large hunter which went okay until we got into the wood on Hosey Common. We were standing around waiting for some people to catch up when this beast decided to chuck me off.

I landed hard on my bottom and sat there feeling extremely sorry for myself. I was told not to be so wet and to get back on, which I did. We set off, me with a sore bottom, and we'd hardly gone a few yards before the horse decided to bolt straight down the narrow path through the trees.

'Bloody hell!'

'Don't swear, Ludo,' I said. 'It's not attractive.'

'Sorry, Grandpa. What happened then?'

'I couldn't stop the bloody thing, so I hung on for dear life, half clinging round its neck, with twigs and branches whipping across my face, until suddenly we burst out onto the playing field of the village school.'

'Golly, what a relief,' said Tug.

'If only it had been. There were goal posts at either end of the field and this horse was hurtling toward one of them. I thought it was going to go straight underneath and I'd be done for.'

'And did it?'

'Apparently not. The next thing I knew I was waking up in a darkened children's ward of the local cottage hospital. I can only think that the horse must have slipped on the hard, icy ground, and thrown me off onto my head.

'The doctor wasn't as worried about my head as he was about my back. He was right, as it turned out. I had cracked a vertebra and spent the next few weeks lying flat out on a hard bed at home without a pillow. In the middle of which the King died. Nothing to do with me, you understand.'

Ludo sniggered politely.

'It isn't funny,' said Tug.

'Ironic, though. I got back to school in time to watch the funeral on a tiny black-and-white screen in the dining room. Just as the cortège reached Paddington Station en route for Windsor, I got a terrible tummy pain and that evening ended up in hospital again with appendicitis.'

Tug said, 'I always thought ironic meant something happening which isn't what's expected, and everyone thinking it's quite funny.'

'Right,' I said.

I was going to go on and explain that the whole point of the story is that things that happen to you in childhood can affect you when are old, but decided that this was something that they should discover for themselves. They almost certainly wouldn't have believed me.

Two Stops from Barking

I had a friend who, if he considered someone to be a bit dotty, referred to him, or her, as Upton Park – i.e., two stops from Barking.

In order to catch the full flavour of this somewhat elliptical nomenclature, you would need to be familiar with a) the District Line on the London Underground and b) the phrase 'barking mad'.

Not that the people he ever described in this way were clinically insane. The merest hint of eccentricity would, in his mind, deserve this sobriquet. The fact that he was as eccentric as anyone I knew never occurred to him. Had *he* known someone who never wore shoes or socks inside the house, whatever the temperature, or who, cycling along the towpath of a tributary of the Thames, managed to plunge headlong into the river, Upton Park would have been the first words that came to his lips.

Sadly, he died far too young, so his friends were deprived of the opportunity to witness his eccentricity at its apogee. The reason I am so sure that we had not seen the best of him in this regard is because of a piece I read in the *New Scientist* some years ago, stating that odd and eccentric behaviour increases with age.

This finding, based on an extensive study by the Professor of Mental Health at Imperial College, London, Peter Tyrer, must be as much of a comfort to countless oldies as it is to me. Needless to say, I am not in the perfect position to list the sort of behaviour which my family and others categorise as eccentric – mainly because it's their word against mine, but also because in most cases I have no idea what they're talking about.

What, for instance, is so odd about letting insects out of the window? Or eating horseradish sauce with pork? Or darning one's socks?

By an odd coincidence, Professor Tyrer once had a job as Spike Milligan's gardener, and was able to observe an eccentric *sans pareil* at close quarters.

Could Spike, one wonders, have been the original inspiration for the Imperial College study?

Professor Tyrer has suggested that some might make a virtue out of oddness, and Spike, perhaps more than any other entertainer, was as well known for his personal idiosyncrasies as he was for his writing and performing – though on the whole there was very little distinction.

Often there was method in his apparent madness. While many of us who hate slaloming our way along London streets on casually abandoned dog dirt have thought of doing something about it, but have done nothing about it, Spike did. If he saw a dog making a mess and the owner walking on blithely, he would pick up the offending material in an envelope, follow the owner all the way home and post the stuff through their letter box.

In case of problems, always go to the top was one of his mottoes, and in the event of the milk not being delivered he'd be straight on to the chairman of United Dairies.

Other eccentricities had less practical usages – such as sitting in his office on the top floor of his house in London and sending a telegram to his wife in the kitchen saying 'Where's my bloody lunch?'

It is arguable whether a man whose life had been one long round of weird and wonderful behaviour of Spikean proportions could possibly get any weirder with age, though there are plenty of examples of older men, and women, who became increasingly expressive of their traits of eccentricity.

William Cavendish-Scott-Bentinck, 5th Duke of Portland, who succeeded to the title in 1854 instead of his older brother, who had died young, never liked talking to people and was reputed to have refused to see anyone in person except his valet. He even attached a door to the side of his bed so no one would know whether he was there or not, and every day he had a chicken posted through the letter box and ate half for lunch and half for dinner.

For him, the best way to get away from everybody was under ground, so he built around a dozen large tunnels below his estate at Welbeck Abbey. Some were tall enough to grow trees, others wide enough for horses, and he even managed to make a space large enough to accommodate a ballroom, an observatory and a billiard hall.

The older he got, the more reclusive he became, until he ended up living in five small rooms, each with its own lavatory, painted pink.

Despite his determination to remain invisible, he was

immortalised by Kenneth Grahame as Mr Badger in *The Wind in the Willows* – arguably one of the most familiar and best-loved characters in English fiction.

More eccentric still was Sir George Sitwell, the father of Osbert, Sacheverell and Edith. Harold Acton described him as 'the strangest old bugger you ever met'.

He was obsessed with all things Italian, and spent months in Italy in full evening dress, collecting baroque artwork and studying Renaissance gardens. A compulsive hypochondriac, he never travelled without a huge case of medicines, each one of which he carefully mislabelled in order to deter anyone else who might think of using them.

Visitors to his home, Renishaw Hall in Derbyshire (refashioned by him in the Italian style), were startled to be confronted by a sign at the entrance to the estate saying, 'I must ask anyone entering the house not to contradict me in any way, as it interferes with the functioning of my gastric juices and prevents my sleeping at night.'

He also invented a musical toothbrush and a tiny pistol for shooting wasps.

Eccentric behaviour has always been a trait more commonly found among the old. The young and middle-aged take care to temper any wayward behaviour in order to keep in line with their peers and contemporaries. But one of the greatest joys of growing older is the losing of one's inhibitions and not worrying about saying exactly what one thinks.

An old friend of Mrs Matthew's and a much-loved member of the House of Lords was once asked by a female friend if he and his wife would like to come to dinner the next Friday. He replied that he was very sorry, but that he was busy that evening. She said that perhaps the following Tuesday might be more convenient. He gave the same reply. 'Oh dear,' said the woman. 'Well, how about the following Saturday.' 'Oh, all right,' said the noble lord. 'We'll come on Friday.'

The same elderly peer of the realm was once asked by a rather grand lady if he would be interested in coming for a golfing weekend in Sandwich. 'No,' he said.

They're on Your Head!

One of the great features of advertising agency life in the sixties was the long lunch.

While outsiders usually presumed they were just an excuse for so-called 'creatives' to get out of the office and enjoy vast amounts of food and drink at someone else's expense and generally enjoy themselves, wiser heads were convinced that the action of eating and drinking engendered good ideas: among them David Puttnam, who started life in advertising before moving into the film industry and producing, among other classics, *Bugsy Malone*, *Chariots of Fire* and *The Killing Fields*.

When he went to Hollywood in the eighties to be head of Columbia Pictures, he recorded how delighted he was that the time-honoured commissary system, in which writers and artists and directors lunched together every day and exchanged ideas, was still very much part of studio life.

'That third cup of coffee or that extra glass of wine,' he remembered, 'can often trigger thoughts and ideas.'

Having myself often eaten in the sixties at La Trattoria Terrazza in Romilly Street, Soho, a favourite of writers, artists and film directors, I understood his enthusiasm.

I would like to think that I, too, was once bubbling over with witty headlines and sparkling ideas for new ad campaigns for cornflakes or washing-up liquid. Fifty years later, however, the only thing that triggers me at the dinner table is the sudden inability to remember anybody's names or how the subject arose in the first place.

At a lunch party last weekend I was trying to think of the man who sculpted the famous head of Lawrence of Arabia. Don't ask me why.

'He was also a painter,' I said. 'Quite famous. You'd know his name immediately.'

The fellow guest to my right, an elegant and cultured woman of approximately my age, was doing little better.

'Henry Moore?' she hazarded.

'No, not him. Not quite as famous.'

'Epstein?'

'Epstein was very famous. He did a memorial in Battersea Park to soldiers in the First World War.'

'Epstein did? I didn't know that.'

'No, the man I'm trying to think of did. What *is* his name?'

'Antony Gormley?'

We both gave up in the end. I remembered the name in the car going home. Eric Kennington. As if it mattered anyway.

Helpful clues are equally elusive. Here's an old joke. Two old geezers are sitting in a lounge waiting for their tea to appear. 'Where did you go for your holiday this year?' one of them asks his pal. The man can't for the life of him remember. 'What's the name of that stuff that grows on buildings?' he says. 'You mean moss?' says his friend. 'No, that's not it. It's a sort of plant. Climbs up walls.' 'Wistaria?' 'More common

than that. It's green. You see it on the walls of stately homes.'
'You don't mean ivy?' says his friend. 'Ivy. That's it,' says the
man. He turns and shouts in the direction of the kitchen,
'Where did we go on holiday, Ivy?'

Few things strike fear into elderly hearts more than dementia, or, worse still, Alzheimer's. Never mind the thought of
getting it; the word alone is enough to chill the blood.

Memory is one of the few things that distinguishes us from
animals, and having a good memory is a skill to which we all
aspire – whether in the school room, or at a reunion of some
kind, or at a pub quiz. And yet few subjects cause general
merriment more than absent mindedness, memory loss and
mental deterioration.

*There are three main ways of telling if you are getting old:
memory loss and . . . I can't remember the other four.*

'I'll be forgetting my own name soon,' my mother would
announce cheerfully if she couldn't remember an old friend's
telephone number, or where she'd put her glasses.

Seven times out of ten they were on her head.

'Let's all go round the bend,' she'd say, and we'd all laugh.

Luckily she never did. She never forgot my name either, or
my brother's, and even though I saw her rarely in the last few
years of her life, she always knew who I was and still made
jokes about her occasional absent-mindedness.

My father certainly went a bit doolally towards the end for
reasons that were not fully explained, but not so much that
we found ourselves grieving for him prematurely.

Whether being a bit confused counts as dementia I have
no idea, nor do I really want to know. I don't believe either
of them had Alzheimer's, which may be my way of trying to

persuade myself that I won't get it either, but who knows? These days even the tiniest and silliest incident can have the mental alarm bells tinkling.

I was walking down the street in London where we were living at the time when a car drew up next to me and a man stuck his head out the window and said, 'Olumpia?' 'Sorry,' I said, 'didn't quite catch that.' 'Where Olumpia?' he said.

The fact that he was in a left-hand-drive car, combined with the strong Gallic accent, produced in me an overwhelming desire to prove that some of us in England can speak a foreign language. I crouched down beside him and suddenly found myself launching into fluent French. Well, I say 'fluent'; I was certainly making the sort of *bof* noises French people make when they are speaking and shrugging my shoulders and saying '*alors*' a lot, and my detailed instructions on the quickest and easiest route to Olympia clearly made perfect sense to him. Just to make sure, I repeated the entire itinerary.

So effusive was his gratitude and so continental was I feeling by this stage that I think I even told him what a pleasure it was to welcome a fellow European to our capital and that I hoped we might meet again one of these days.

Off he went in exactly the direction I had given him and I continued on my way feeling really rather pleased with myself.

It was as I was turning the light out in bed that evening that I realised I had sent him to Earl's Court.

I don't think that was a symptom of anything more worrying than sheer absent-mindedness – or possibly just one of those moments of mild confusion that can happen to anyone of any age and at any time.

I once heard of a man who was standing in a line-up

waiting to shake hands with the Queen, and got himself into such a state of confusion over how he was to bow and how to address her, and how much pressure to put on the royal hand, that he ended up curtseying to the Duke of Edinburgh.

The older one gets, the more often one finds oneself doing something idiotic and thinking, Oh God, here we go; but is there any point in worrying about things one hasn't got when there are all too many things one already has? Age-Activated Attention Deficit Disorder, for one. This is not unlike the thing that some children have when they can't concentrate properly during lessons, but more embarrassing.

You know how it is: you set off to do one thing, then get distracted and start doing something else, which leads to a third thing, and before you know what, you end up not doing what you set out to do originally, but having done lots of things you never intended to do, wondering where the day has gone.

In case you have no idea what I'm talking about, have a look at a sketch about AAADD on the internet, directed by Steve Pemberton, about a woman who sets off to wash her car and is on her way to the garage when she notices a pile of letters on the kitchen table. She starts to sort them out into bills and junk mail. She throws the junk mail away and decides she might as well pay the bills. She goes to her desk . . .

Hang on. Why on earth am I bothering to tell you the plot when you can look it up yourself? I can guarantee it will give you one of the biggest laughs you've had all day – until you suddenly remember ten seconds in that you've forgotten to worm the cat.

You're Not Really Going to
Tell That Story Again, Are You?

There are a number of variations on the theme: WIB (Words in Bedroom); WOD (Words on Doorstep); WIT (Words in Taxi); WIP (Words in Parking Space); WOP (Words on Pavement); WAD (Words at Dinner Table) . . .

Different couples have their favourites, but arguably the most popular is WIC (Words in Car). These frequently take place on the way to someone else's house for a social event of some sort, and they are prompted by a variety of reasons: faulty time-keeping ('I thought you said we were leaving half an hour ago'); faulty map-reading ('I *said* you should have turned left at the traffic lights'); faulty choice of in-car entertainment ('Not the bloody *Archers!*'); faulty clothing ('I do think you might at least have put on a tie'); faulty introduction of conversational topics that have proved highly contentious in the past and are guaranteed to add tension.

It is also the one favoured by the better mannered. Any guest who has arrived earlier at a dinner or a party (i.e., on time) can recognise the symptoms of WIC the moment the subjects enter the room: the forced smiles; the over-stated bonhomie; the sideways glances ... But at least everything that needs to be said has been said in the privacy of a moving and distant vehicle. Or has it? WICs tend not to spill over into the event in prospect, though WAD is not unknown in even the smartest circles.

(Footnote here: Although WICs of all kinds are open to couples at any stage of their married lives, they do seem to be more popular with the oldies who enjoy nothing better than raking over old coals – not just in the car, but sometimes in public too.)

Examples of WAD are the exception rather than the rule, but we have all witnessed them in our time. They usually begin with a softly spoken, light-hearted rejoinder from the wife (or the husband), along the lines of 'Darling, you know I don't like you talking about my cooking like that.' Or, with a light laugh and a conspiratorial glance round the table, 'Honestly, my mother would *never* have said anything like that about French people.' Or, more simply, between gritted teeth, 'We agreed not to bring this up in front of other people.' The perpetrator, encouraged perhaps by fellow guests, finds himself pursuing the matter and, before you know what, it's WAD in no uncertain terms.

WAD can often arise when one partner takes it upon him or herself to assume that because he/she has heard an anecdote or joke several times before, fellow guests should be deprived of the pleasure of hearing it for the first time.

'Darling, you're not really going to tell that story again, are you?'

This situation arises more often with the older generation

than with the young, and for a number of reasons: she thinks the story is unsuitable for the present company; he has forgotten he told the same story/joke to the same people only recently; he messed it up then and chances are he's going to mess it up again.

What very few fail to realise is that even if other people have heard a story before, they will probably have forgotten the punch line, or indeed the whole thing, and will, at worst, listen to it politely and, at best, enjoy it all over again.

People like nothing better than a repeat performance of a good anecdote.

Did anyone ever complain when Pavarotti sang 'Nessun Dorma' for the twenty-seventh time?

More to the point, when a couple who have been together for years are getting on a bit, it is not unusual for each to assume that the other is the one who is getting absent-minded and quite capable of not knowing whether he or she has told a particular story before – possibly to the people with whom they happen to be dining; whereas both are equally guilty of absent-mindedness, and what the one who tries to save the other's blushes has failed or forgotten to take into account is that the older people get, the more likely they are to have dreamed up a different version of the original story, and that the one he or she is about to (as the other thinks) repeat, will in fact come out fresh minted and, with luck, unrecognisable.

But these are fine details when set against the real problem, which is that not only do wives (and to a less extent husbands) get bored with the same stories, but that the chances of an old geezer coming out with an observation, or a *mot bon* or *juste* or merely a snippet of information which isn't boring becomes increasingly rare.

We lesser mortals might find it inconceivable that Jean-Paul Sartre and Simone de Beauvoir ever uttered a boring word in all the years they cohabited, but I bet they did. I bet she said, 'If you tell that story about how President de Gaulle didn't understand your best existential joke one more time, I'm going to scream.'

All couples who have been together for a long time get bored with each other, however beguiled and entertained they might be most of the time – especially if, like Jean-Paul and Simone, they are sitting in separate rooms thinking and writing all day. They also have silly arguments about the most trivial things, usually because one or other of them is going deaf and gets the wrong end of the stick.

Deafness is often a great source of amusement to those who are lucky enough to have kept this particular faculty intact.

There's a joke about a man who is convinced his wife is going deaf, but can't be absolutely certain and doesn't know how to find out. He seeks professional advice from his doctor, who suggests that next time he passes the kitchen and sees his wife busy preparing a meal he should enquire in a normal voice, 'What's for dinner, darling?' If she doesn't reply, he should take a step or two into the room and ask the same question. If that doesn't produce a result he should move closer and closer, asking the same question as he goes. That way he can judge just how deaf she is.

He does as the doctor suggests and is understandably concerned that however near he gets to her, she still doesn't reply. Finally, he is standing right behind her. He tries one more time. 'What's for dinner, darling?' To which she replies, 'How many more times? Chicken!'

Those who can't hear quite as well as they used to and complain that the sound system on their television set is not of the highest quality and that people these days don't speak clearly and precisely enough are finally faced with two choices: continuing to refuse to admit they have a problem, and carry on pretending they can hear perfectly well when they obviously can't, or press the subtitles button.

Most, however, will bite the bullet and buy an expensive hearing aid – preferably one of those types that is so discreet as to be almost invisible.

Few wish to flaunt their disability. One who made no bones about it and used his deafness as a social weapon, often to make people feel uncomfortable, was Evelyn Waugh. Though only sixty-two when he died, he acquired two large ear trumpets. One, in tortoiseshell, was a gift from the Duchess of Devonshire, which one could attach to one's head, thus allowing one to eat and drink. The late Alexander Chancellor, whose daughter is married to Waugh's grandson, once tried it out and declared that he could hear better through that than he did through the state-of-the-art Swiss-made electronic aid which had cost him two thousand pounds.

Waugh's cousin, Claud Cockburn, described how he used his trumpet to withering effect at a Foyle's Literary Luncheon, at which Malcolm Muggeridge was the main speaker. Within a minute of the unfortunate victim rising to his feet, Waugh had unscrewed the trumpet from his head, removed it from his ear, placed it on the table in front of him and sat gazing intently at his plate.

Muggeridge was completely thrown. Having spoken for less than half his allotted time, he sat down, whereupon Waugh picked up the trumpet and started adjusting it once more to the listening position.

His second trumpet, a plated copper job, English-made, came up for sale in March 2017, supported by a letter of provenance from Waugh's mischievous son Auberon: 'I have sent you a disgusting object . . . You may be able to identify it as a telescopic ear trumpet as used by my father in his later years . . . It may be of some whimsical interest to an obsessive collector.'

The guide price was £1000 to £1500.

Eleven O'clock, a Fine Night,
and All's Well

It still almost beggars belief that when my mother was a year old, the Wright Brothers got the very first heavier-than-air powered aircraft off the ground. When she was twelve, a company called Aircraft Transport and Travel stuck two passengers in the fuselage of a former military biplane called the Airco DH4A and flew them from Folkestone to Ghent, thereby launching Britain's first fixed-wing airline. When she was sixty-seven, Neil Armstrong climbed down out of the *Eagle* lunar module and stepped onto the surface of the moon.

Almost as hard to believe is that only three years before I was born, on 26 August 1936, the Movietone News commentator Leslie Mitchell announced the arrival of television at Radiolympia with the words, 'Good afternoon, ladies and gentlemen, it is with great pleasure that I introduce you to the magic of television.'

On 25 November, the first regular service began transmitting for two hours a day from Alexandra Palace.

On 29 July 1948, at the age of nine, I saw my first television pictures on a tiny set belonging to someone in our road, as King George VI opened the 14th Olympic Games at Wembley Stadium.

My sole entertainment when I was growing up was the wireless – *Children's Hour* at first and later *Dick Barton, Special Agent*. Occasionally in the holidays we were taken to the local cinema to see films like *The Wooden Horse* and *The Cruel Sea*, and, on very rare occasions, to London to a children's show. *Archie Andrews' Christmas Party* was a particular favourite. Most of the holidays were spent mucking about on our bikes, playing cricket in the garden in the summer, swapping comics and reading books.

My parents did not buy a television set until well into the sixties, and, like many of my contemporaries, I struggle with computer technology and the internet. Social media is beyond me and always will be.

Small wonder, then, that I am as out of touch with the life of instant communication that my grandchildren take for granted – indeed, with more or less every aspect of their lives.

Being still at school, they cannot imagine that a day will come when they will be as out of touch with the way of life led by their children and grandchildren as I am with theirs, and that they will find themselves struggling to describe a world which seems, even to them as they look back, unbelievable, and that many of their closest friends now will be but a hazy memory.

I am made ever more conscious of this when I receive the latest bulletin, either through the post or via the internet, from my school. I always look through the old boys' section in the hope that I might recognise a name of a friend I lost touch with some time back in the mid-fifties and discover what he has been up to all these years.

It rarely happens. Most of the names and faces who are keen to share their news, or who have been at a reunion dinner or some such, belong to comparatively new alumni. Where mine have all gone is something of a mystery. I imagine a lot have been summoned to the great headmaster's study in the sky; indeed the majority of the very few names that ring a bell are in there only because they have died. As for the rest, I can only assume that they share my view that they haven't got much news to impart and that, if by any chance they did have, there aren't enough people reading the old boys' news who would remember them. In fact, the only time I have ever come across a contemporary in recent years, the name has meant nothing.

Nor is there the slightest hint in anything contained within the bumph about the school that even nudges my memory. There are tales of extraordinary expeditions to remote corners of the globe, of amazing careers in finance and science and industry that we could never have begun to imagine in our day. Boarding houses with names I don't recognise are celebrating their half-century. New buildings devoted to art and music and drama and sports are being opened in locations I never knew existed. And then there are the girls.

If the boys of today shine, the girls are shining even brighter. They all look so grown up, apart from anything else. If one of them had, for some reason, suddenly turned up in our midst, we would, for all our macho talk, have been terrified, gone bright red and made our excuses.

Someone who was at the school at the same time as me is

making a collection of memories of the place in the fifties, to which I have contributed some – though, reading through them, I find myself wondering, as I do when reading anything I have written about my youth, how much of it is true, if anything.

Can it really be possible that we all slept in rows of iron-framed beds? And that a night watchman, straight out of Dickens, would patrol the school buildings and, as he reached the archway in the yard outside our windows, would call out in lugubrious tones, 'Eleven o'clock. A fine night. [Or a wet night, depending.] And a-a-a-ll's well'?

And that when we were new boys we had to fag for our elders and betters, and polish their shoes and Blanco the belts of their corps uniforms, and make tea for them and toast their crumpets.

Our lives seem in retrospect to have advanced little from that at Rugby, as described in *Tom Brown's Schooldays*. As a new boy, I was assigned a desk in the old Victorian junior hall, which was, in its rugged way, my home for two years. The senior boy was the Captain of Hall and his lieutenants were called Top Fires, because in times gone by they were allowed to sit next to the coal fires which, years ago, provided the only heating in the place.

It's a wonder someone didn't take it into his head to light one and roast a few junior boys over it.

More astonishing still is that the most senior boys in the school, the House Captains, were entitled to beat junior boys for some misdemeanours. And if a boy committed a really serious crime, he could be sentenced to a school beating, which meant standing bent over a table in the school library while every one of the dozen so school monitors, equipped with a cane, would run the length of the room and deliver a mighty whack across the unfortunate victim's buttocks.

Why did we not rebel, like the boys in the Lindsay Anderson film *If...*?

Why did our parents not complain at what amounted in extreme cases to child abuse? I can only assume a) that it was a phrase with which, in the early fifties, they, and everyone they knew, were totally unfamiliar, b) that if you spend good money sending your child to a reputable school, the people in charge must know what they're doing and it's not the parents' business to interfere, and c) that we had never thought such atrocities worth mentioning.

Having heard evidence from a number of fellow pupils who, were they of school age today, would be receiving therapy and their parents large sums by way of compensation, one of the witnesses concluded cheerfully that at schools like that in those days you either sank or you swam, and if you swam it gave you a confidence that stood you in good stead.

And in most cases it did. I think. I hope.

Swiss Cheese

'Grandpa,' said Ludo. 'Can I ask you something?'

'Ask away,' I said.

My response was not quite as relaxed as it might sound. Given that most of the time he is with us is spent staring at his iPad like a rabbit hypnotised by a stoat, it came as quite a surprise that he uttered anything at all, let alone asked a question. What subject could be important enough that he could not find the answer on his screen? I hoped it was not going to be the kind of request that might put me on the spot with his mother. Money for something that had already been kicked into the long grass, perhaps.

'What's a finishing school?'

'Well, they don't really exist any more, but they used to be schools in places like Paris and Switzerland which taught young women social graces and polite behaviour.'

'What? You mean like not farting in the middle of lunch?'

'They were certainly taught how to get in and out of a sports car without showing their knickers.'

'You're joking.'

'You could be forgiven for thinking so. But it's true. When I was growing up in the fifties and sixties there was something called society, which didn't mean the community, like it does now, but the world of the upper classes. And if a young woman wanted to be accepted and invited to dinners and dances, and find a nice young man to marry, she needed to know the rules for polite behaviour.'

'My friend Boris's granny was laughing at one of his jokes during lunch and she suddenly farted. Really loudly.'

'Either she didn't go to a finishing school, or she suffered from flatulence.'

'What's flatulence?'

'I understand the technical term is an accumulation of gas in the alimentary canal.'

'Is that serious?'

'It can be at mealtimes.'

'Or if you're meeting the Queen.'

'Exactly. You never know. Anyway, why the sudden interest in finishing schools?'

'It's just that I was looking up your Wikipedia entry, and it says there that you taught in a girls' finishing school in Switzerland.'

'Ah,' I said. 'That's a bit of an exaggeration, to tell you the truth. I did teach at a school in Switzerland for a year, but it was really an international language school. The majority of the pupils were indeed girls, but they had come from various European countries not in order to learn how to walk up and down with a book balanced on their heads, or how to cook *crème Anglaise*, or how to climb out of a sports car without showing their knickers, but to learn French, German and

Italian, and do a bit of skiing in the winter. If asked, I do sometimes claim it was a finishing school, because that way it sounds a bit more exciting.'

'Not really,' said Ludo.

'Right,' I said.

'Anyway,' he said, 'what did you teach?'

'English and general behaviour. Mainly towards myself.'

'Was it fun?'

'Quite. I've rather forgotten, to tell you the truth. It was over fifty years ago.'

'Golly.' There was a pause. 'What was the best bit about it?'

'Meeting Mick Jagger,' I said.

It happened on a warm Friday afternoon in 1964, in the Montreux Casino where I found myself at a recording of *Ready Steady Go!* – the ITV rival to *Top of the Pops.*

Why it should have occurred to anyone to record an English TV pop show in Montreux, of all places, I can't imagine. Nor can I remember how I came by a ticket. Or even what persuaded me to use it. I had never been a big pop music fan. I must have had an hour or two to spare, and thought, Why not?

I hadn't been in England for a year, so when these four young blokes with ridiculously long hair started twanging and banging away, while a fifth one with skinny legs pranced up and down like Max Wall, shouting into a microphone, my first thought was that something must have gone terribly wrong back home.

'Who are this lot?' I asked someone.

He looked at me as if I was mad.

'The Rolling Stones, of course,' he said.

'Never heard of them.'

I can't remember who else was on the bill, but after the show was over the Stones' manager, mistaking me for a journalist perhaps, introduced himself as Andrew Oldham and asked if I'd like to have a drink with the boys.

I looked at my watch.

'Actually, I'm a bit pushed for time—'

'Just a quick one,' he said.

'As long as it's quick,' I said.

The boys and I stood around awkwardly in the bar with Cokes in our hands (Coca Cola in those days), all of us clearly wondering what we were doing there. I have no idea what we talked about, if anything.

Finally, I put my glass down, gave the singer's scrawny arm a friendly squeeze, and said, 'Stick at it, boys. I'm sure you'll do very well one day.'

I arrived back at the school in time for tea and revealed where I had spent the afternoon. For the first, and only, time in my life, I was mobbed by a bunch of teenage girls. Some of them actually screamed.

Later that week, the local rag reported that the Stones had celebrated their night in the Montreux Palace Hotel by taking a pair of large scissors and getting to work on the carpet on the main staircase.

Forty years later I met Mick in a box at Lord's. The place was full enough of famous faces as it was, but then in walked Jagger and his girlfriend at the time, the immensely tall, very beautiful and, as it turned out, very tragic L'Wren Scott.

The English are odd about celebrity. If they happen to find themselves in a room with someone really famous, they tend to pretend the person isn't there and go to extraordinary lengths to avoid him or her. As I did with Mick and L'Wren. Didn't want to seem pushy, you understand. What would the most famous rock star in the world have to say to a free-lance journalist who has occasionally appeared on *Quote* ... *Unquote*?

Quite a lot, as it turned out. About the cricket, mainly. Totally, in fact. Indeed we nattered away so much that I began to wonder if he wasn't monopolising me.

But all good things come to an end, and finally Mick had a helicopter to catch, and I was keen to get to the 414 bus before the crowd got there.

I could just have said goodbye, nice to have met you, but no: the temptation to place myself was irresistible.

'Actually,' I said, 'you won't remember it, but we've met before.'

'Oh yeah?' he said.

'Montreux Casino. Summer of 1964. *Ready Steady Go!*'

His face crinkled into a beam of remembered pleasure.

'The band's first trip abroad,' he said.

'Don't think it didn't show,' I said.

'Yeah. We didn't behave very well.'

'Words "carpet" and "Montreux Palace" ring a bell?'

'Oh, that.'

'I was out there teaching in a girls' school at the time,' I told him.

'Lucky you,' he said.

There was a pause.

I said, 'I remember I had a drink with you in the bar. I told you to stick at it. I was sure you'd do well one day.'

'Well, you got that right, anyway.'

I suppose that even to one so unversed in the pop culture (I'm more of a Cole Porter man), it should have come as no surprise that my prophecy on that afternoon was fulfilled in no uncertain terms. What I would not have predicted was that that skinny little bloke should not only have been still at the top of his game over half a century later, but that at the age of seventy-three he would become a father for the eighth time.

I can see that there are still countless girls who would give their eye teeth to have Mick as father to their child, but I can't help wondering what he will be making of it all. Not just now. Babies are always a joy at any age, but in fifteen years' time, when little Deveraux Octavian Basil is at his most teenage-tearaway stage, how Mick will cope at eighty-eight. Join him, perhaps?

Even his oldest daughter will be sixty by then. The only member of the Jagger family anywhere near Deveraux's age will be Mick's great-granddaughter, Ezra Key, and even she'll be two years older than her great-uncle.

What persuades a man, any man, to have a baby with a woman sixty-four years younger than him? Is it just because he can? I don't mean physically, or financially, but because he's Mick, and when you're someone like Mick, you can do whatever you like, whenever you feel like it.

He's surely got beyond the stage of wanting to prove some-thing: that he can still pull, that he is still fertile, there's still plenty of gas in the tank . . . Perhaps he just loves babies, and not just anybody's, but his own.

Delighted though one is to know that old age is no bar to a family life normally reserved for couples the age of his . . .

well ... granddaughter, there are precious few of us willing or able to follow Mick's example. Indeed, one's first thought might be for his health. He must be tired enough after a gig as it is without being awake half the night with a squawking infant. But then, of course, we remember that's never going to happen to a man who can afford to hire the best nannies in the world. An army of them, if necessary.

More of a concern to those of us whose days of child-rearing are long lost in the mists of memory and whose concerns are focused on two generations ahead, are what it's going to be like for young Deveraux to have a father who is the age of one's grandfather. How will that go down with his school pals when he turns up for parents' evening or the nativity play? Will the old man be the object of enormous attention – something that is normally anathema to children? But then, of course, Daddy isn't any old father. He's one of the most famous people in the world.

To us he is, but will he be to his son's friends in seven or eight years' time?

Perhaps I am worrying too much. He is far from being the only old-age dad that I can think of offhand. The Dean of Canterbury when I was at school there in the fifties, Dr Hewlett Johnson, known as the Red Dean for his pro-communist leanings, seemed to all of us boys as old as Methuselah with his polished brown pate and his fluffy white locks, and at eighty-something he wasn't far off. What amazed us more than his age, though, was that he had two daughters, Keren and Kazia, who were about the same age as most of us.

Whether they had any misgivings about having such an elderly father we never knew, since in those days pupils at boys' boarding schools were forbidden to associate with girls on pain of expulsion. Even if they were the Dean's daughters.

Having old parents per se may not be the problem some of us oldies might suppose. What we wouldn't wish for them is parents who are old-fashioned – something that Deveraux Jagger need have no qualms about, but which clearly bothered Woody Allen.

'My parents,' he wrote, 'were very Old World. They come from Brooklyn, which is the heart of the Old World. Their values in life are God and carpeting.'

Oh, by the way, I've suddenly remembered something else Mick said about our Swiss encounter. 'You do know, don't you,' I said, 'that in those days Montreux was the gay capital of Europe.'

'Not on my watch it wasn't,' said Mick.

Pop Off

My hopes of being invited on to *Desert Island Discs* are looking thinner by the day. But one lives in hope, and it never does any harm to look from to time at one's hypothetical list of records on the off chance of a call, and I see from my last – as I thought it, eclectic – collection of musical gems, that I have not included a single what you might call pop record.

Anyone listening in to this (hypothetical) programme and hearing me described as 'the veteran' (i.e., over sixty) broadcaster, journalist, poet, whatever, could be forgiven for thinking that I had led a sadly sheltered life: that I had never taken to the dance floor in a night club, or slept in a yurt in a muddy field in Somerset, or attended a single pop concert.

Ludo has never quite recovered from the revelation that I have not seen a single *Star Wars* film. This is not some form of affectation. I may sometimes pull the 'old buffer who confuses Adele with Fred Astaire's sister of the same name and is astonished to hear that she is still working at the age of a hundred and twenty-one' trick, but I never watched *Star Trek* either and feel I am none the poorer for it.

He may be doubly dumbfounded to learn that I once, as I think I have hinted earlier, had a reputation as something of a mover on dance floors here and there in the heyday of the twist, that my interpretation of 'It's Now or Never' in the style of Elvis Presley caused a riot at a coming-out dance in Little Venice, and that I once went to a Bob Dylan concert at Earl's Court. But I am not what you might call a dedicated pop fan.

Having caught the very beginning of the Beatles and then immediately moved abroad for a year, I seem somehow to have missed out on the pop scene (*qv* my 1964 encounter with the Rolling Stones).

So, for the purposes of not letting my grandchildren down, what would be a suitable record in that category which I might choose to listen to on a regular basis while bouncing around on my own on a sandy beach in the South Pacific or wherever? I suppose I could play safe and choose a Beatles number, though that might have people groaning over their Sunday-morning elevenses: 'Oh, not "She Loves You" *again*. Can't he think of anything more interesting?'

Occasional forays into *Sounds of the Sixties* on Radio 2 have often had the effect of transporting me back to a flat I once shared with a couple of blokes and the odd passing bird (sorry, young woman) just off Baker Street, where *Top of the Pops* was a highlight of our communal week – largely on account of Pan's People.

Anyone not of our generation who happens to see an old black-and-white recording of *Top of the Pops* on BBC 4 could be forgiven for taking one look at the audience members jigging listlessly around in front of the bands and thinking that life in the sixties wasn't quite as swinging as they had been led to believe. Unless, that is, they catch sight of Pan's People. Just mentioning the name gets me going.

For all I know, I may be missing the chance to see them all in action again – Dee Dee and Flick, Babs and Louise. Maybe those magical legs that we all fell in love with and the dance moves that had our eyes out on stalks are still shown from time to time in some nostalgic programme or other, but I have an awful feeling that, like so many delights that I remember with such fondness from my youth, they will turn out to be a disappointment.

I don't know if it is a common affliction of old age that the pleasures of the past suddenly acquire a disproportionate degree of significance in one's ageing mind, but there was a recent period in my life when, for reasons that I can't explain, I started to fill my Christmas and birthday present lists with all manner of nostalgic nuggets that I felt that I not only had to experience for myself one more time, but that I was sure my family would appreciate just as much as I once had.

Ever since I first went to Paris to stay with my gassy youngest aunt in her tiny rooftop apartment in the sixteenth arrondissement when I was fifteen, I have had a love affair with French culture – enhanced in no small degree by the arrival of the Nouvelle Vague cinema of Truffaut, Godard, Chabrol and Rohmer at the Scala in Walton Street in Oxford.

One of the great pleasures of my bizarre year in Switzerland was being able to speak fluent French (with a terrible Swiss accent), and to listen to and understand the songs of Charles Aznavour and Hugues Aufray and Alain Barrière and

223

Françoise Hardy and Sylvie Vartan, and see French films and spend time in Paris during the holidays, pretending not to be English.

For some reason I got it into my head a year or two ago that Truffaut's *Jules et Jim* was the best film I had ever seen and I felt sure Mrs Matthew and my two sons, both in their mid-thirties, would agree. So I bought a DVD off Amazon, and we all settled down to one of the longest films I can ever remember seeing.

Were there quite so many scenes in which nothing much happened and then nothing much happened again? It had its moments, and so did I. But a lot of emotional water has flowed under the cultural bridge since I lay on the floor of my digs with a beautiful girl called Somebody Something and we listened breathlessly to Georges Delerue's luscious score on the 45rpm record I had just acquired.

Thoughts of Pan's People jogged memories of some of the songs I still remember from my *Top of the Pops*-watching days and still sound as good today as they did half a century ago: 'You've Lost that Loving Feeling' by the Righteous Brothers; 'Baby Love' by the Supremes; 'Waterloo Sunset' by the Kinks; 'I've Got to Get Out of this Place' by the Animals; 'Glad All Over' by the Dave Clark Five; 'Will You Still Love Me Tomorrow' by the Shirelles . . .

Crikey – and there I was saying I was never into pop. What I really meant was that I haven't been into pop since the Beach Boys sang 'Good Vibrations'.

Ever since then I have been lost in the musical wilderness, straining to catch a single word that anyone sings of songs that, to my untrained ear, sound extraordinarily similar. The crowds that sway and swing along to Coldplay never seem to have the slightest difficulty with the words, but of course they know them all already.

I have a couple of friends who have kept up with the pop scene, but many more go to Glyndebourne and Covent Garden. Perhaps we are all missing something without realising it. Perhaps the songs and the artists who my children think are the bees' knees really are.

I recently read somewhere that children who listen to rock music do better in their exams. Now they tell us.

I have a friend who is utterly bewitched by André Rieu. She will go anywhere for one of his concerts. She once went to Maastricht to hear him. That's how keen she is.

His genres of music range from classical and classical cross-over to easy listening, and he and his 1666 Stradivarius and his Johann Strauss Orchestra have his audience swooning with every item in his romantic repertoire – from the Intermezzo Sinfonico from *Cavalleria Rusticana* to 'Somewhere Over the Rainbow' and from 'Nessun Dorma' to 'Volare'. For ladies of a certain age, he is their Robbie Williams.

I am surprised that some of our elder statesmen of radio and television have not seen that there is a fortune to be made from giving the old dears what they want. And the old geezers.

The idea of squashing into Hyde Park for a concert by the Kings of Leon would never cross my mind, but I'd pay good money to hear *Gyles Brandreth Sings Noël Coward* in Budleigh Salterton, and join in with the chorus in 'Mad Dogs and Englishmen'.

Whatever Happened to Whatsisname?

If I should meet thee
After long years,
How should I greet thee? –
With silence and tears.

Alan Coren and I spent many hours over many lunches thinking back over our lives, wondering if we were making the best of what was left and whether any good can ever come of trying to revive old friendships long since lost, abandoned or forgotten.

The conversation usually ended with Alan quoting those lines from Byron's poem 'When We Two Parted'.

He, Byron, was speaking of a love affair that evidently ended badly; of cold kisses, and grief, and broken vows. But all too many attempts at personal reunions have a habit of falling short of expectations.

In Jim Jarmusch's film *Broken Flowers*, retired computer magnate Don Johnston, played by Bill Murray, would seem to be confident he knows what life is about and has no greater ambition than to sit around the house watching old movies. But then he receives an anonymous letter breaking the news that he is the father of a nineteen-year-old son. Encouraged by his neighbour, he sets out on a journey to visit all his old girlfriends who might be the most likely candidates and find out which of them is the mother.

Each encounter brings with it yet another dose of embarrassment, reminding blokes of my sort of age of the shock any of us might feel on seeing someone we knew decades before and discovering how old they look and realising we must look just as old to them.

We may think we have lots of questions to ask each other, memories to share and old jokes to pull out from the bottom drawer, and for a while we do. We are certain we made the right decision and we feel the long years of absence melting away. But then, all too soon we find we're both running out of jokes and reminiscences, and we're left wondering what we're doing there and why we bothered.

It's fine for the young. When Ludo's school friend Hedgehog came back after a couple of years living with his family in Australia, I asked him if he thought they would still be friends.

'Why wouldn't we be?' he asked.

I said that quite a lot of time passed since he had last seen him, both had had all sorts of different experiences, made new friends, acquired new tastes, and both might have changed.

Ludo said, 'Actually, he hasn't changed a bit. He's just the same as he was when he went away.'

If only, at my age, one could say the same. Meeting old friends can often seem like a visit to a theatre. Once-familiar figures look as if they have just spent time in the make-up department and the theatre wardrobe, and have emerged wearing heavy padding – especially in the stomach area – bald wigs, false teeth in a variety of styles and colours; their faces heavy with wrinkles, jowls and hanging flesh, their bodies bent over limps and wobbles, supported by all manner of props, from glasses and sticks to hearing aids and peculiar voices.

Happily, for the most part, however much one's sixties flatmate may look like the name part in a village-hall production of *King Lear*, the fundamentals are still there, concealed beneath the crumbling surface.

I recently met a friend from my college who I hadn't seen for over fifty years. Correction: I had seen him – or at least I thought I had seen him – in an online photograph of his daughter's wedding. It was his unusual name that had first caught my eye, but clearly it was not the man I had once known: an older brother perhaps, or a distant cousin, or just someone else who happened to have the same name.

The man I knew was tall and slim and handsome, with boyish, unruly hair and a careless smile. The one in the photograph was obviously tall, but carrying much more weight, was very thin on top and wore a worried scowl beneath beetling brows.

A couple of months later I found myself behind just such a man in my local surgery, waiting for a prescription. He gave his date of birth – the key that seems to unlock everything that needs to be known about a National Health Service patient. It appeared he was only a little older than me. And then he gave his name.

He stood upright and turned round. It was the man in the photograph.

'Philip?' I enquired.

'Yes,' he said, clearly puzzled.

'Do you remember me?'

It took some time, but finally he agreed that he did. We shook hands. He smiled. And at that moment, the disguise – the plump features, the bald pate, the heavy eyebrows, the scowl – melted away and the slim, carelessly coiffed young man I had known all those years ago was suddenly standing there in front of me again.

We chatted for a while as we made our way to the local Boots to collect our pills, and discovered a few facts about each other's careers; mentioned a few names of mutual friends, agreed to keep in touch, and went our separate ways.

Did we keep in touch? No. Will we still try? I very much doubt it. We registered that we were both still alive, which is really the best one can hope for in these situations. Beyond that, no tears, but a continuing silence, for which we are both, I daresay, grateful.

Whether he would have acknowledged me had I not told him my name is a moot point. It isn't so much whether I have changed out of recognition that concerned me as much as whether I had ever made any impression of him in the first place.

The thought might never have crossed my head had I not remembered a story the *Sunday Times* journalist Alan Brien would often tell against himself. Following the end of his first marriage he went to live in New York, where he became friends with Leonard Bernstein and his wife Felicia. He was a frequent guest in their apartment and attended the famous party on 14 January 1970 that the Bernsteins hosted for ninety prominent figures in the arts and media to raise funds for twenty-one Black Panthers accused of planning to kill police officers and blow up department stores.

Back in England, Alan found a new girlfriend, and when he heard that Bernstein was to conduct a concert in St Paul's Cathedral he wasted no time in buying a couple of tickets.

Discovering that there was to be a reception afterwards for the great man in the Deanery, and thinking to impress the girlfriend, he suggested they should go along so that he could introduce her. She protested that they had not been invited, but he assured her that, as an old friend, they would have no trouble getting in.

He was as good as his word. Entering the room where the reception was being held, all they could see was a mass of backs. As they moved towards it, the crowd divided like the Red Sea and Alan and the girl walked through it until they came to face with the great man.

Alan stepped forward and embraced him. 'Lenny,' he murmured

Bernstein took a step back, held him at arm's length and gave him a long, hard look. For several seconds he said nothing; then he spoke.

'Who the fuck are you?' he said.

Words of Wisdom

I was peeling a few contemplative potatoes one Sunday morning recently while listening to the omnibus edition of *The Archers*. Well, not listening as such. I've made it sound as if peeling potatoes and *The Archers* go hand in hand for me on a Sunday morning; as if it's part of my weekend routine. 'Oh goodee: time for potatoes and *The Archers*.'

I know a lot of people for whom half of Borsetshire are close personal friends who they bump into twice a day and again on Sunday, and for whom their everyday lives, however boring, are of deep personal interest.

Not me. I am not a fan – unlike Mrs Matthew, for example, who is. Big time. I occasionally catch snatches of the programme if I wander into the kitchen or wherever she happens to be listening, or has been and has suddenly remembered something she should have been doing in another room and has walked out, leaving it on. Which is more or less what happened that Sunday.

So while it is true that, technically speaking, I was listening to *The Archers*, I was only vaguely aware of these people nattering away behind me about this and that while I was concentrating on doing a first-class job on the Maris Pipers. A lot more was coming off, as it were, than was going in.

But then suddenly I heard this voice saying, 'That's what grandparents are for, isn't it?'

I may not be as intimate with Peggy and Brian and Pip and Josh and Ruth and David and their friends and relations as some, but one thing I feel sure of is that they – the older ones, anyway – are deeply rooted in good, solid British common sense. Hence the pricking up of my ears and a keen desire to know what words of wisdom a senior Ambridgian might have to offer on the subject of grandparents.

The plotline in question, when followed later on BBC iPlayer, revealed that Kirsty was having a baby with Tom, but didn't want to live with him, and his parents, Tony and Pat, had decided that their son was going to be 'a great dad as long as they work it out between them'. Which, at that time, they seemed to think they would.

'We'll love that child just as much, regardless of whether they're living together or not,' said Tony. And then came that line again: 'That's what grandparents are for, isn't it?'

Is it? Except in very unusual circumstances, it is taken for granted that grandparents love their grandchildren, whether the parents are married or not, or living in the house or not. It's what nowadays is known as a given. But I can't help feeling that there is more to grandfatherhood than merely exuding affection. I mean, surely one's meant to do things with one's grandchildren, isn't one? Take them to the Science Museum, tell them amazing stories about one's adventures on the roll-ercoaster of life, show them how to swing a golf club, teach them to recognise all the different birdsongs, introduce them to favourite authors, start them on a stamp collection . . . ?

Well, yes and no, it would seem – at least if one of my wise chums' advice is anything to go by.

One summer, not very long ago, when the grandchildren were still children, I was complaining to him that I had suggested all manner of treats to them, none of which had met with anything more than a mumbled 'Do we have to?'

He was on to it like a hawk on a titmouse. 'Listen,' he said. 'What are you doing trying to organise their lives? That's what fathers do. You're a grandfather. Your job is to smile benignly, offer the occasional word of wisdom if called for, and generally make them feel at home so they want to come back again.'

Words of wisdom, eh? Sounds simple enough – except that I seem to have arrived in my mid to late seventies feeling almost exactly as I did fifty years ago, and knowing even less.

When I say 'feel', I mean mentally. Physically speaking, I sometimes 'feel' about a hundred and eight, especially first thing in the morning.

Going to bed, I'm as perky as any man half my age: my back doesn't ache, my legs aren't stiff, my eyes are bright, and my head is clear. Getting out again seven hours later (if I'm lucky), I feel as ancient as the hills. Indeed the actual process of throwing back the duvet, swinging the legs across and down, and rising to my feet requires what Robert Harris describes in his novel *Conclave* as 'a precise sequence of planned manoeuvres'.

Actually, getting out of bed is a doddle compared with rising to one's feet from a deep sofa or armchair. Provided the bed is high enough, that is. You simply place both feet on the floor, push down and, with a bit of luck, you're suddenly standing there, wondering what the next move might be and whether you're ready for it. If the bed is a low divan type and, when you place your feet on the floor, you find your knees are at waist, or even chest, height, then you can reckon you've got your work cut out to attain anything like a standing position. A certain amount of serious rocking to and fro is often required before you can gather sufficient momentum to hurl yourself forward and upwards. Even then, it might take two or three goes before success is achieved. Getting out of an armchair demands a similar technique, and a helping hand can come as a huge relief.

Once on your feet, progress can be slow, not to say painful, and a certain amount of grunting and groaning is called for as you totter towards the bathroom (yet again; you have almost certainly made the short journey several times already in the small hours). The simplest movements – pulling on the dressing gown, easing the feet into the slippers, drawing back the curtains – are only slightly less challenging that the Labours of Hercules.

During such moments I feel about as old as the High Lama of Shangri-La in *Lost Horizon*. And probably look it.

Being still quite fit for my age, I can usually reckon it's only a matter of moments before all the parts begin to move again and, indeed, an hour later the machine is, if not well oiled, then certainly back to the serviceable normality of yesteryear.

This is something of a delusion. Just because I can walk along to the kitchen unaided and without uttering a small groan with every step, it does not mean that I am a latter-day Benjamin Button.

One quick look in the mirror very quickly puts paid to any thoughts of magical rejuvenation. My problem is that I simply cannot reconcile my physical state with the conviction that, mentally, I am only just getting started. Inside my head I feel that I am exactly the same person that I was on the day I began my first job and that I have acquired none of the wisdom that I assumed to be an essential ingredient of early-onset dotage.

I had fondly imagined that with my grey hairs would come wise advice I could usefully pass on to my children and grandchildren. Yet now that the moment has come, I find I have nothing to offer but banalities.

This has come as a huge disappointment to me. After all, what is a grandfather for if not to pass on grandfatherly counsel culled from a long life of experiences, good and bad?

I was recently chatting with Tug about careers in general and hers in particular. She currently has ambitions to be a doctor. Though being a very talented musician, she also wonders whether a career in music of some kind might be on the cards.

I don't suppose she was expecting me to do anything other than sit there and listen, but I felt that a word or two of advice would not go amiss.

'In my experience,' I heard myself saying, 'careers are things to look back on rather than to look forward to.'

She stared at me. 'Well, that's not much help,' she said.

Put like that, it was at best a pompous platitude and at worst a thoughtless put-down. What I was trying to suggest is that, however carefully we plan our lives, they turn out to be full of surprises.

All of us dream at some time or other of a fantasy place we

can escape into – a Neverland, a Narnia, a world reached by a low door in a wall which, if opened, can change our lives for ever.

It happens, famously, to Charles Ryder in *Brideshead Revisited*, when Sebastian Flyte invites him to Brideshead by way of escaping the 'rabble of womankind' up for an Eights Week ball.

Ryder is uncertain at first ('for it was foreign ground'), but accepts.

I was in search of love in those days and I went full of curiosity and the faint, unrecognised apprehension that here, at last, I should find that low door in the wall, which others, I knew, had found before me, which opened on an enclosed and enchanted garden, which was somewhere, not overlooked by any window, in the heart of that grey city.

I had a similar experience at university when an acquaintance invited me to lunch at his parents' home one sunny Sunday in the middle of term.

The journey wasn't quite as glamorous: instead of an open two-seater with a basket of strawberries, a bottle of Château Peyraguey and a teddy bear, we travelled on a Green Line bus. But the pretty, extended cottage set in a large garden with a swimming pool by a wood at one end was to me every bit as thrilling as the 'new and secret landscape' of Brideshead. And the lunch *en plein air* and the food and the wine and the jokes were a world away from the modest Home Counties life which was all I had known up till then.

As we were leaving later that afternoon to catch the bus,

my friend's father shook my hand and said, 'Do come and see us again. You may not want to see us, but we should always like to see you.'

The house was to become my second home; my university chum my best friend; and his family my second family. I always wanted to see them, and they always seemed pleased to see me.

It might have seemed rather fanciful to suggest to a fifteen-year-old that such a door could be out there somewhere, waiting just for her and that she should take care not to miss the opportunity of opening it and possibly finding an enchanted place of her own. But my suggestion that she should keep her eye open for all opportunities, social and professional, to recognise them when they presented themselves, and not let them pass by without investigation, could be helpful.

In Charles Ryder's case, it all ended in tears. Like him, we may well discover that one day the low door in the wall is suddenly shut, and the enchanted garden has gone. But that is no reason not to look out for it.

All this may not be the pearl that falls into some grandchildren's laps, and I may still feel that I am not blessed with the abundance of wisdom I had expected at my age, but perhaps I need not worry too much. It would appear that I am not alone. The great American satirist and cultural critic H. L. Mencken felt much the same as I do. 'The older I grow,' he wrote, 'the more I distrust the familiar doctrine that age brings wisdom.'

So, if not wisdom, what does it bring? Apart from wrinkles. My hero Garrison Keillor suggests that it might come totally open handed. 'Sometimes age comes alone,' he concludes. But, then, Garrison is a man who famously deals in the downbeat. What one needs are words, if not of reassurance, then at least of good sense. Who better than Hemingway to give it to you straight between the eyes. 'No,' he wrote, 'that is the great fallacy: the wisdom of old men. They do not grow wise, they grow careful.'

And if that's not the perfect segue into my broken hip, I don't know what is.

The Old Man and the Knee

I am currently working on a treatment for a sequel to *Falling Down*. It's called 'Falling Over' – a portrait of a world in which hardly a week goes by in the lives of the over-seventies without news coming through of yet another victim of the stumble, the trip, the misplaced step, the slippery slope, or the unwise leap for the overheard smash.

Orthopaedic surgeons must be hugging themselves with undisguised glee and thumbing through catalogues for super-yachts as their secretaries add yet another name to their operating lists.

Accidents are nearly always idiotic and the results all too often catastrophic. Silly accidents incurred by elderly acquaintances in recent months include the woman who stepped down from a Range Rover in a petrol station just as her husband edged forward over her foot and parked on it; the man who was suddenly overcome by the desire to kiss his wife, pulled in to the side of a country lane and was in the act when his knee released the handbrake and the car drove smartly into a tree; and the keen tennis player who somehow managed to put her foot through a hole in the net and break her hip.

Which is exactly what I did a few years ago: not playing tennis, but skiing. To be precise, getting off a chair lift in order to continue skiing.

I have, in the course of a fifty-year skiing career, witnessed a fair number of idiotic cock-ups and mini-disasters on slopes all over the world.

In Méribel I once saw a bulky middle-aged man who had not been concentrating in a chair lift queue and had somehow contrived to plonk himself down on a seat that was already occupied and was being carried up the mountain on a young woman's lap. In Champéry, an amply built woman fell off a button lift and was stuck with her legs spread-eagled, unable to move, so the man coming up behind had no alternative but to ski up over her bottom and back and continue blithely to the top. Skiing cross-country in Norway, a bunch of us stood at the top of a wide expanse of sloping countryside, at the bottom of which was a lake and in front of it the only tree in sight, and watched as a skier descended nervously towards the lake and went straight into the tree.

My own accident – in Switzerland – was only slightly less idiotic, though it still resulted in a hip replacement in the nearest hospital, a second one when that one went wrong, and several years of pain, assorted physiotherapy and all-round irritation.

On the positive side, it has meant that I have been able to commiserate, advise, visit and generally bore all my friends who, willingly or unwillingly, have had to have new hips.

How on earth did people manage before John (later

Sir John) Charnley took up a post in the Orthopaedic Department of Wrightington Hospital near Wigan shortly after the war?

Bust your hip or suffer agonising arthritis before then and you'd have no alternative but to put up with it and shut up.

It was inconceivable that someone might one day be able to cut you open, hack through all the underlying muscles, remove your femur, replace it with a metal one, stich up all the muscles and sew you up again, then send you home, and that within days you'd be swinging around on a pair of crutches with the grace and élan of an acrobat in the Cirque du Soleil, suddenly free from some of the worst pain known to humans.

But that is exactly what thousands of old geezers and old ladies have done to them now every day of the week and give it little more thought than they would a nasty dose of flu.

Sir John is rightly honoured for pioneering hip-replacement surgery, though he wasn't the first to have a crack at it.

The first recorded attempt to replace a hip was in 1891 when a surgeon in Germany by the glorious name of Themistocles Gluck used a femoral head made of ivory, attached with nickel-plated screws, plaster of Paris and glue. It wasn't until 1940 that Dr Austin T. Moore performed the first metallic hip replacement in the Columbia Hospital, South Carolina. In 1952 he introduced the Austin Moore Prosthesis, which is still in (rare) use today. Ten years later, Sir John produced the design that is, with small variations, used to this day – namely a stainless steel one-piece femoral stem and head, and an acetabulum (i.e., the concave surface of the pelvis) made of polyethylene, attached to the pelvic bone using bone cement.

For those who have been suffering for years from arthritic hips to the extent that they cannot move without intense pain, the operation is nothing short of a miracle. Discomfort from the actual operation apart, patients suddenly find themselves pain-free for the first time in years.

For those like me, who had perfectly good hips in the first place and were looking forward to having both in prime condition for years to come, the replacement is not always such an unqualified success.

The operation that was performed in the Swiss hospital near the resort where I stupidly broke the damned thing by stumbling as I got off a chair life and falling, quite gently, onto a nearby pile of snow, was carried out, as far as I can make out, by whichever surgeon happened to be on duty that lunchtime. I can distinctly remember someone mentioning that my insurance wasn't up to paying for the top man, and while the operation was in progress – with me wide awake behind a sheet, numbed by an epidural – there was quite a lot of lively chat coming from the business end, which suggested that the whole thing was a doddle. So much so that when the sound of hammering got louder as they bashed the pointed stem into the remains of my old femur, I couldn't resist joining in with some modest banter.

'Who's in charge down there?' I called out. 'Michelangelo?'

'This is a very serious matter,' came a stern female voice, which suggested that if I didn't pipe down it would be the worse for me.

Which indeed it turned out to be when I had to have the whole thing done again. The surgeon who operated on me in London presented me with the old prosthesis. It is surprisingly heavy and could either be used to knock burglars on the head or to make a few bob on eBay from someone who didn't mind wearing my ex-leg.

The other disadvantage for hip-replacees of all stripes is that going through the airport security is always going to set the bleeper off, and even though you mutter the word 'hip' at the man as he moves remorselessly towards you, you know that nothing is going deprive him of the pleasure of running his hands over your torso and inner thighs, and inside your waistband – sometimes rather more probingly than one might think necessary.

It was another skiing accident that resulted in the tendons in both my shoulders being torn and having to be replaced, but otherwise I am equipped with more or less all the joints I was born with.

Unlike many of my contemporaries, I have been able to stagger thus far supported by my own knees, though there are times when I wonder if they really *are* the best knees I'll ever have.

Not that any of those substitutions and subtractions are necessarily associated with old, or even late middle, age. Moreover, all those I know who have experienced physical changes to their bodies have recovered and I'm glad to say are still with us.

But darker fates await, preying on my dreams like Freddy Krueger lookalikes who are bored with slashing teenagers and have decided to try their skills on a few oldies. Time was when they were somewhere out in the garden, lurking in the bushes; but any day now they will be in through a window left carelessly open and lurking, invisibly, in the shadows in the corner of the room.

Who knows when they will decide to strike, or why.

And yet both my grandmothers lived to a great age, never having seen the inside of a hospital or had a day's illness in their lives. I have a feeling they made them tougher in those days.

Gone Tomorrow

Call it bad luck, or bad habits, or what you will, but the fact remains that ten years ago I lost three of my best friends. None of them was in very good shape – thanks to a variety of physical and mental problems – but, even so, never once did I imagine we would not be enjoying old age together. I lost another old friend three years ago. Like the others, he had suffered not only from ill health, but from being in his sixties.

The sixties are clearly a dangerous decade. I have no gerontological knowledge to back up this assertion, but I have often heard it suggested that the quicker and more safely one makes it through one's sixties, the better one's chances of moving easily into old age. From which one hopes one will move equally easily towards the exit.

One of the few advantages of failing to make the cut before the biblical norm is that it will earn you a lot more sympathy than if you hang about.

'He was far too young,' people will say. One of the most annoying things about dying at any age over seventy is that no one will ever say you were too young. The best one can hope for is 'He had a good innings.' It sounds reassuring enough, but very much depends on how you got out. Carelessness? Did you hang your bat out to a ball that was clearly swinging away and get an edge? Did you misjudge a delivery, dance down the pitch and try to hoick it for six over midwicket and get caught just short of the boundary? Did you get clean-bowled by a yorker? Or a googly? Or did you carry your bat right through the entire innings and leave the field applauded by your team-mates, waving it modestly at the crowd?

More to the point, how much did you score in your lifetime? Will it be enough to ensure a decent turn-out at your funeral?

At this point, I don't mind admitting that while embarrassment at my latest faux pas (especially those within Mrs Matthew's hearing) can keep me awake more than anything else in the wee small hours, thoughts of mortality come a close second.

Julian Barnes entitled his memoir of mortality *Nothing to be Frightened Of* – more out of reassurance than from conviction. He is scared of dying – or at least certain phases of it – as much as the next man.

'I fear,' he writes, 'the catheter and the stairlift, the oozing body and the wasting brain.' Nor does he mind admitting that 'I expect my departure to have been preceded by severe pain, fear, and exasperation at the imprecise or euphemistic use of language around me.'

I remember thinking when I was desperately cramming for my finals at university, and praying for a last-minute miracle, that although one knew there was no way out of it, one reassured oneself with the thought that we were all in the same boat and everything would come out all right at the end. Not unlike death, I thought. Except for the bit about everything coming out all right.

More than half a century later, I find myself having similar thoughts. About death, I mean. If my dear departed friends can face it and go through with it, so can I. There won't be much chance of a wild, congratulatory post-event get-together on the pavement with one's friends covered in foam and streamers, pouring champagne over their heads, but at least we'll all have been through it together.

Any help? Probably not. There isn't a lot anyone can say to make the idea of dying seem more palatable.

Mark Twain penned some of the more reassuring words on the subject: 'I do not fear death. I had been dead for billions and billions of years before I was born, and had not suffered the slightest inconvenience from it.'

Nice one, Mark, but that still leaves an awful lot of things one might miss: the driverless car; not knowing if Camilla ever became Queen; never again walking with a dog on a warm autumn afternoon in Kensington Gardens; not discovering if a new set of golf clubs would make a difference to your game; never knowing whether anyone thought anything of you, or remembered you affectionately after you'd gone.

Indeed, a fulsome and preferably amusing obituary is the least one can hope for. Time was when the lives of the great and the good were celebrated in the obituary pages of the broadsheets with nothing more than dispiriting *curricula vitae* and the obits desk was generally thought of by news-papermen as being the journalistic equivalent of Outer Siberia.

Which was why, when Hugh Massingberd took on the job of obituaries editor of the *Daily Telegraph* in 1986, many of his friends regarded his appointment with, as he put it, 'a mixture of pity and contempt'.

Under his watch one discovered what people were really like through lively descriptions, character sketches and anecdotes. So successful were these celebrations of lives of all sorts that many of them were anthologised, and continue to make entertaining and, frankly, rather enviable reading.

Just to read a list of someone's occupations was often a joy in itself. The 3rd Lord Moynihan, for example, was a 'bongo-drummer, drug-smuggler and police informer, though he enjoyed other areas of expertise, such as "professional negotiator", "international diplomatic courier", "currency manipulator" and "authority on rock and roll".'

The 'erratic Irish-born restaurateur' Peter Langan would 'regularly launch himself at customers he found, usually for some unfathomable reason, offensive. Often he would pass out amid the cutlery before doing any damage, but occasionally he would cruise menacingly beneath the tables biting unwary customers' legs.'

As for the High Court judge Sir Melford Stevenson, famous for handing down stiff sentences, just a handful of caustic courtroom observations were enough to tell you as much as you needed to know about the man.

Of a husband in a divorce case he said, 'He chose to live in Manchester, a wholly incomprehensible choice for any free man to make'; and he acquitted a man of rape with the words, 'I see you come from Slough. It is a terrible place. You can go back there.'

The only surprise is that the writer failed to mention that his house on the Sussex coast was called Truncheons.

The internationally famous medium Doris Stokes, known as 'the Gracie Fields of the psychic world', also earned a memorable appreciation in the obituary pages under Hugh's editorship.

Described by William Donaldson in his *A-Z of Rogues, Villains and Eccentrics* as 'appearing on stage in a high-street frock and with her hair styled locally', she would pass on reassuring messages from family members on 'the Other Side' – though occasionally her lines would become slightly crossed.

'He went very quickly,' she told one member of her audience. 'He was ill for six months,' came the voice from the auditorium. 'Well, he went very quickly at the end, lovey,' retorted Doris.

Of Sir Rupert Grayson, Bt – guardsman, King's Messenger, seaman, writer and publisher – his obituarist wrote, 'In every circumstance "Rupe" Grayson manifested a talent for survival: it was said of him that even if – unlikely contingency – he had tried to drown himself in the Thames he would have washed up alive in the Grill Room of The Savoy.'

One would dearly wish to be remembered with equal fondness and humour, though one's life is likely to be summed up in less glowing terms. Like that of the theatre producer, director and actor Charles Cowper Ross, on whose headstone in Hampstead Cemetery are his own words:

What will be said
When I am dead
Of what I used to do?
They liked my smile?
I failed, with style?
Or, more than likely, 'Who?'

It is perfectly understandable that people choose comforting words for family and friends to read at funerals – a little something to make everyone feel that losing their husband, wife, parent, friend isn't really quite as bad as they had thought. No wonder Henry Scott Holland's words are top of the pops:

Death is nothing at all.
I have only slipped away to the next room.

The religious-minded will, equally understandably, condemn this kind of stuff as trite and sentimental. For the young, it could, and possibly does, provide comfort; the middle-aged have usually heard it so many times that they no longer give it any thought, if they ever did. And, anyway, for them dying is still a long way off.

Those of us for whom it is, or at least could be, just around the corner, are also looking for some kind of explanation; something altogether more practical that will lift us from the gloom and pessimism that old age can so often bring with our failing strength, our fading sight, and our waning appetite for food, for adventure and for life.

Writing about old age in *Somewhere Towards the End*, the

ever wise and brisk-minded Diana Athill believes that it is the presence of the young which should and can sustain us. Being pessimistic, she says, is boring and makes our final years even more dreary than they already are.

> Whereas if, flitting in and out of our awareness, there are people who are *beginning*, to whom the years ahead are long and full of who knows what, it is a reminder – indeed it enables us actually to feel again – that we are not just dots at the end of thin black lines projecting into nothingness, but are parts of the broad, many-coloured river, teeming with beginnings, ripenings, decayings, new beginnings – are still parts of it, and our dying will be part of it just as these children's being young is, so while we have the equipment to see this, let us not waste our time grizzling.

Quite right. There's no point in fussing. One must get on. Yesterday I made some more subtle changes to the pro- gramme – the service, rather – I have proposed for my funeral. I had planned on doing one for a memorial service, but then I thought, What if no one turns up? How embarrassing would that be? Not for me, of course, but for my family and the few ultra-loyal friends who had taken the trouble to be there.

On the other hand, people of my age enjoy nothing more than a memorial service – regardless of how well they knew the subject, if indeed they knew him or her at all. I went to one only the other day in a large country church which was jam- packed, and so was the village hall next door, where dozens more were following proceedings via a relay system. I had it on good authority that the attendance figures were a parish record – which was saying something since the church was six hundred years old. Roughly a year for every member of the congregation.

I said to a woman who had served with the deceased on the PCC for twenty years, 'I know she was a popular figure in the WI and on the local council and meals on wheels and so on, but could she possibly have known as many people as that?'

'I shouldn't have thought so,' she said. 'But you know how it is. No one wants to miss a memorial service. There's no better way to meet old friends and make new ones. I have a friend who goes to at least one memorial service a week and has barely exchanged two words with the people whose lives she is celebrating.'

If I have learnt one thing in my life it is that there are always exceptions to every rule, and though planning my own memorial service may not be the worst idea I've ever had, on the grounds that I am not going to be there anyway, I am sufficiently embarrassed already by the thought of three people sitting in the front row wondering if they've got the date wrong, that I am only too happy to leave the whole thing up to someone else.

If anyone who has nothing better to do feels like arranging one for me, that's fine, but they shouldn't count on my leaving a note in a drawer describing what I'd like to have happen and who I would like to have to say a few words of appreciation.

Mind you, I'm not expecting to be at my own funeral either, but friends and family and people I know will be – or should be – and I'd hate to think of my wife and children arguing about what hymns they thought I liked, or what I'd like to hear people reading out of the Bible or whatever if by some extraordinary quirk of nature I happened to be there.

Quite recently I added Bette Midler singing 'The Wind Beneath My Wings' to my putative list of *Desert Island Discs* (fat chance), mainly because it would be the perfect opportunity to talk about Mrs Matthew, and how I wouldn't have got anywhere in life if it hadn't been for her, and actually, I thought it might go well at my funeral too. Not quite sure where. TBA at this stage, I think.

Having made out the list of possible runners for the service, if not the riders, I'm going on the assumption that the event is going to take place in a church: probably the one just round the corner from where we now live.

The plan, according to my latest will, involves a service to be taken at my local church by the erstwhile vicar – an old school friend and the man who first taught me, aged sixteen, how to smoke. (It was a pity he didn't also remember to mention that if you hold a fag between your fingers with the back of your hand facing downwards, they will very quickly develop a nasty suntan which your father will almost certainly spot the moment you arrive home for the holidays.)

There'd be a brisk rendering of 'For All the Saints'; a couple of thoughtful readings; a few kind words from somebody; more lusty singing of 'For Those in Peril on the Sea' and 'The Day Thou Gavest'; and an exit accompanied by the Tommy Dorsey version of 'Swing Low, Sweet Chariot'. The vicar will then accompany me to the cremmy for the committal, returning to join the stragglers for the booze-up.

But then I had a better idea.

How would it be if I were to arrange a second half of the

funeral that would be rather more in keeping with me and my life than a gloomy crematorium in Mortlake, even if it had once hosted Robin Day, Lord Longford and Tommy Cooper? Not all on the same day, of course.

My first thought was a scattering: from a fishing boat off the Suffolk coast, where we have had a family house for the last forty years. Then I remembered a story that the *Punch* cartoonist Geoffrey Dickinson told about scattering his father's ashes on Southport golf course and how the wind suddenly got up and changed direction so that the ashes were sprinkled all over the mourner's clothes; and how he had to go into the nearest branch of Achille Serre and ask if they could please clean his father off his overcoat.

Which was when I had the brilliant idea of inviting all my friends to meet by the sixth green on Aldeburgh golf course, where the golfers among them would be handed joke golf balls to be driven in the direction of the River Alde, bursting in the air and scattering *moi* over the rough, which is where I have spent so many happy, if frustrating, hours of my golfing life.

I feel sure nothing could go wrong – though, having said that, cock-ups can occur even at the most traditional events. At my mother's funeral, in a village on the Isle of Mull, we were all preparing to head to the cemetery high on a nearby hill, looking out over Rhum and Muck, when the driver of the hearse found that however many times he turned the engine over he couldn't get it to go, so we all had to set to and bump-start it down the drive.

Worse things have happened at funerals. The story goes that Dorothy Parker and husband Eddie arrived early at a crematorium in New York where a friend was already there in his coffin on the dais whence he would finally say farewell to this world by sliding through the curtains.

Gossiping about their late departed chum while casually examining the device on which he lay, Dotty came across a small button at the side. 'I wonder what this is for,' she said and pressed it, whereupon the coffin disappeared through the curtains and into the oven.

The late Garry Shandling, the creator of Larry Sanders, suggested a far simpler solution during an episode of *Comedians in Cars Getting Coffee* with Jerry Seinfeld. He said that what he wanted for his funeral was a boxing referee to stand over him and do a count, and at 'five' just wave it off and say, 'He's not getting up.'

A Wonderful Way to Go

An inevitable drawback to getting older is a nagging anxiety about how it is all going to end. A fatal heart attack? A knockout stroke? A long, one-sided battle with Alzheimer's? A stupid accident? In one's sleep? The possibilities are endless. So, one fears, are the consequences.

One tends not to give it much thought if one is feeling chipper – as I am today, as it happens, enjoying a second cup of coffee, looking forward to a few holes of golf with a friend, and noticing out of the window that the rain has almost stopped. Thoughts of mortality are a lot rarer in daylight than at three o'clock in the morning. (Is it any coincidence that it's in the hours just before dawn that most people die?)

Woody Allen clearly devoted plenty of thought to the subject if the large number of wisecracks attributed to him are anything to go by. 'I'm not afraid to die,' he once famously wrote. 'I just don't want to be there when it happens.'

There is one way of achieving the latter and that is by conking out so suddenly and unexpectedly that you barely have time to notice. I speak from experience – not of dying, you understand, but of knowing what sudden death could be like and how it's nothing to worry about, for the simple reason that you haven't got time.

I was out skiing with a party of friends in Switzerland about twenty years ago. The sky was blue, the snow was fresh, the piste was empty, the views were great. We had come down from the top of the mountain, bashing our way through the steepest and toughest slope in the area, and had come to an easy path leading to a gentle incline and all was well with the world. I suddenly felt one ski catch something beneath the snow and suddenly I was heading fast for the outcrop of rocks and ice rising to our left. I had time for one thought: This is not going to end well. The next thing I knew I was lying flat on my back on the snowy path, with blood pouring from my head and our guide leaning over me asking what I had eaten for breakfast.

I was lucky to get away with it. The doctor in the village put fifty-two stitches in the back of my head – luckily in an area where the skull is at its thickest. An inch or two to the left or right and I could have been a goner, or a vegetable. As it was, I ended up with a large scar (the one that disqualifies me from having my head shaved as a fashion statement) and the stirrings of a plot for a thriller.

Had I bought it that day, I have no doubt people would have comforted themselves with the thought that at least I went doing something I enjoyed. 'What a wonderful way to go,' they would have said. Or words to that effect.

The same thought occurred to me when the news broke that a game old boy of seventy-two, one Ralph Hubbard, had been killed on the Cresta Run. He was only the fifth person to die since this three-quarters-of-a-mile-long track of sheet ice was opened in St Moritz in 1885.

I can't think this can have been of great consolation to him, or to his partner and children who were standing nearby at the time, but having once spent a morning watching Cresta Runners in action I am astonished that the figure is so small.

It isn't just the fact that the riders are hurtling head first at speeds of up to 80 mph down a narrow gully of ice on gradients of up to 1 in 9, being hurled from side to side through bends with names such as Battledore and Shuttlecock (anyone coming off at this point becomes an immediate member of the Shuttlecock Club), but that all this is done on something only slightly larger than a tin tray.

Mr Hubbard would appear to have been a veteran of this terrifying experience, which Clement Freud once described as 'the ultimate laxative'. He (Mr Hubbard, that is) had qualified as a 'top rider' – which meant that he started from the very top and had travelled down the Cresta no less than two hundred times. But no amount of expertise and experience had helped him when something went badly wrong and he ended up with a broken neck.

I suppose, as wonderful ways to go, that's as wonderful as any.

My own dice with death, though nothing like as catastrophic as Mr Hubbard's, was less than wonderful. Leaving aside that at the time I was in the prime of life, with three children, it wouldn't have been quite what I was hoping for at that moment. What I really had in mind was a bracing run, followed by a relaxing coffee on the terrace of one of the cafés lower down the mountain. Luckily I had already enjoyed the first part of that and would have plenty of time in the next few days to enjoy the second.

'There are worse things than death,' declared Woody. 'Have you ever spent an evening with an insurance salesman?'

Personally, I'd settle for the salesman. Perhaps not an entire evening, but a couple of hours, as long there wasn't anything good on television. Still, given the huge number of very nasty options available for shuffling off this mortal coil, going quickly while you are at your most contented is not to be sniffed at.

Two friends of mine went recently when they, and their friends and families, least expected it. One – a passionate skier in his late sixties – had just completed a run in perfect powder snow in the Himalayas and dropped dead from a massive heart attack; the other, rather older, died at the breakfast table. Not only had he just eaten his last mouthful of scrambled egg, but he was having a better morning than usual with the *Times* crossword. He'd cracked the anagram at twelve across and had raised his pen to fill in the appropriate letters when off he went, without a word, pen and paper in hand.

Not a bad way to go at eighty-three. Possibly even wonderful. Unfortunately, it's not something that can be easily arranged. However much of a blessing a sudden and painless death might be to the deceased, it's bound to leave a lot of people upset, not to say inconvenienced.

No one wants to make a fuss or embarrass anyone, least of all oneself.

Les Flammes Déjà?

I'm going to drop another name now. I'm doing so only because the story doesn't work quite as well if I don't.

It was 1992 and Alan Coren and I were on our way to Robert Morley's funeral service. I had known Robert and his family for thirty years and, like me, he was a regular contributor to *Punch*.

As we were walking towards Wargrave church, I remarked that it was hard to believe that a man of Robert's wit and charm and huge personality and star quality was no longer with us, that he had gone for good.

'It's because people can't believe things like that that they have religion,' said Alan.

If Robert had any concerns about the afterlife of the everlasting variety, he showed no sign of them. The only time I remember him commenting on the subject was when he said that he was planning to be buried with his credit cards. 'One never knows when they might come in useful.'

He certainly made no plans for his final demise beyond a determination not to leave any money behind for anyone to inherit. As far as he was concerned, he had come into this world with nothing and expected to leave in exactly the same state.

I think that, like a lot English people, he was suspicious of religion – especially when it was called on as some kind of insurance policy in times of emergency. If he thought of God at all, he would have imagined Him as someone not unlike himself, a good travelling companion with slightly left-wing opinions, with whom he could feel on easy terms if he were to find himself sitting next to him at the middle table in the Garrick.

He made no effort to try to find Him. The only times I can ever remember seeing him in church was at weddings and funerals, and it would never have occurred to him, a non-believer, that his own funeral would take not place in a church. Not only is this where traditional English funerals take place, but it is where they do them properly – with proper hymns ('The Day Thou Gavest . . .', 'Abide with Me', 'The Lord's My Shepherd'), sung lustily to a good organ, fulsome and entertaining eulogies, and vicars who knows who they are talking about.

It is many years since I was a regular church-goer. Like many of my generation, I would like to claim that I am a pillar of the Church of England, but like the historian G. M. Trevelyan I am more of a flying buttress, supporting it from the outside. As such, I would like to know that the familiar words of the Church of England funeral service will be ringing out over my coffin in front of the altar, preferably intoned by my old school friend.

He is a man of liberal persuasion, and very much after my

own heart. Once, when a member of the congregation and his wife were exiting from Christmas Day matins and it came to their turn to shake hands, the husband felt it was his duty to apologise for being such a reluctant attender.

'I'm afraid we're not what you might you call regular church-goers,' he said. 'We tend to come only at Christmas and Easter.'

'Well,' said the vicar. 'I call that regular.'

The difference between the Church of England and the Roman Catholics is that for the latter, going to Mass is an obligation which is undertaken in a brisk and no-nonsense fashion, while for us, church-going (at least in its traditional, non-evangelical form) is much more a social occasion – an opportunity for like-minded friends, especially the elderly and the widowed, to meet, sit together and listen to comfortable words and familiar canticles, and chat on the pavements afterwards and meet for a coffee in the church hall.

This sense of warm sociability is passed down through the generations, although for anyone who has ever been to boarding school, or a day school where morning prayers are an essential part of the curriculum, religion and religious instruction have almost certainly been taken seriously.

The service of confirmation and the instruction that preceded it was, in my experience, a time of deep thought and great solemnity. The fact that my teenage years were spent in and around the precincts of Canterbury Cathedral and that we attended prayers every morning in the chapter house and morning service every Sunday in the cathedral quire and evensong in the crypt pretty well ensured that all, except the very sceptical, felt that the Christian religion was fundamental to their upbringing.

Once one had drifted away from the organised world of school, one's religious beliefs became out of focus and seemed irrelevant. One attended the occasional service at university, or at home with one's parents, and one was always happy to hear the familiar words of St James versions of the Bible and the *Book of Common Prayer*.

As somebody once remarked, you can always recognise people who have been brought up in the Church of England; they're the ones who don't need to look at the words to sing the hymns – or indeed the canticles.

'You know your trouble,' a deeply religious elderly friend of mine once commented when I said I was rather depressed, 'you need to get your faith back.'

He had never lost his, and I had always imagined that as I grew older mine would return: that I would need some form of reassurance that my life had not been in vain, that I was going on to a better place, and that I should therefore prepare myself for ... what? Being admitted through the pearly gates by St Peter? Meeting Jesus? Meeting God and sitting at His right hand?

The truth is that, for all the Sunday schools I attended as a boy, and for all the pomp and ceremony of the hundreds of services amid the grandeur of Canterbury Cathedral, and the anthems I sang with the school choir and the shaking of the stained glass in the cathedral windows as the organ thundered, I don't think I really ever acquired much faith.

I remember sitting in a crowded country church, listening to the vicar as he gave a typical Easter sermon concluding with the words, 'And so we know for certain through the Death and Resurrection of our Lord, Jesus Christ, that waiting for us is life everlasting. Amen.'

Hang on a second, I thought. I'm not sure we know anything for certain, do we? Certainly not just because a nice vicar says so. I looked around me at three hundred people, packed into the pews in numbers known only at Easter and Christmas, all looking very solemn, some even nodding in apparent agreement, none displaying the faintest scintilla of doubt.

Is it possible that at the very last I shall acquire the faith that has been missing from life all these years, or will I still be at one with Sir Isaiah Berlin, who I once saw on television pondering the same enigma?

'I would so like to believe in an afterlife,' he said. 'If in all these thousands of years just one person had come back to tell us that it exists, I might. But in the meantime, I must continue to doubt it.'

Woody Allen has similar misgivings: 'If only God would give me some clear sign – like making a large deposit in my name in a Swiss bank.'

For the Catholics an easeful death is guaranteed by a drop of oil and the assertion from the dying that he or she believes, and they are on their way.

The scene in *Brideshead Revisited* when Lord Marchmain, who has returned from exile to his home, is dying, and his priest is trying to persuade his family round his bed that the merest movement of his lips is enough to convince him that the old boy has confirmed his faith is, rightly, one of the oddest and most memorable in all of English literature.

Like Sir Isaiah, I would like to believe as I grow older, but I fear I may be still be as sceptical as Voltaire who, it is said, was on his deathbed when a lighted candle fell onto it and he exclaimed, *'Ah, les flammes déjà!'*

Famous Last Words

There are days when I find myself trawling through the obituary pages in *The Times* or the *Telegraph*, muttering 'Older than me, good ... older than me, good ... oh no, younger than me ...'

Some days are better than others for this harmless and completely pointless form of light diversion, and I am writing this following a particularly ominous week for the mid-seventies crowd. Three big names have gone in just a few days. John Hurt. Alexander Chancellor. Christopher Bland. Seventy-seven. Seventy-seven. Seventy-eight. All three in or around my danger zone.

I'm not entirely sure why I am so concerned. A lot of people die in their seventies, and only the other day someone was telling me a story about a friend of his who had died on the local golf course, which ended with 'He wasn't that old. He was only in his seventies.'

And it's not as if the big three were great friends. It's not like 2007 when I lost three very old friends in the space of nine months and Mrs Matthew lost one of her best friends too. They really *were* all too young. An *annus horribilis* with knobs on.

Perhaps if I were writing this book in ten years' time I might feel rather more sanguine about the constant disappearance of contemporaries. By then, I hope, I will be feeling that I've had the best of it and I won't be worrying about a Pythonesque foot descending out of nowhere and squashing me flat.

That isn't quite what happened to the aforementioned musketeers. All had already been laid low with a variety of potentially killer balls – cancer, hearts, stroke, whatever – but the news that three shining lights have been switched off, just like that, still comes as a shock. We can ill afford to lose them. Or anyone else of their ilk.

Their obituaries spoke of lives richly led, of talent fully deployed, of enviable wit and character, of yet more gifts to be offered to the world. Once again I find myself wondering if I am making the best of such time as I have left to me. I have yet to come up with a reassuring answer. Who ever does?

On the other hand, I can comfort myself with the knowledge that, despite the days and weeks I may have frittered away on humdrum domestic duties and illnesses and traffic jams and black-and-white war movies in the afternoon on Channel 4, the hours I have spent with my friends have never been wasted.

Having read the long and fulsome tributes to the above-mentioned trio, published in the same issue of *The Times* on 30 January 2017, I found myself once again wondering how I could ever have thought that I have made the best of my life.

I can't believe any of them could have had any such misgivings. Oscar-nominated actor and knight of the realm; legendary editor of the *Spectator*; chairman of the BBC, also knighted – I can't imagine them sitting over battered cod and triple-cooked chips in a pub in north London as Coren and I so often did, wondering if they were making the best use of their time. I wonder what was going through their minds as they were on their way out. It seems improbable that even the most famous among us would be devising last words in the hope that they would be good enough to be remembered and widely quoted in future years.

If they were going to come up with a really memorable wisecrack, *aperçu* or *bon mot* of some kind, chances are that they would already have done so.

The internet devotes countless lists of random quotes by the famous, and just a quick look through my commonplace book reveals a few that anyone might be proud of. To wit:

Max Beerbohm at a performance of Peter Pan groaning, 'Oh for an hour of Herod!' An Irish butler waking up a guest in a country house bedroom with the words 'Will I give you the daylight?' And a chance remark overheard at the Chelsea Arts Club: 'She mistimed her lunge, but I managed to knee her into the lake.'

Some of the most famous last words, it turns out, were not actually last words at all. Indeed, in some cases they might never have been uttered at any time by the people in question.

King George V, not known for his sense of humour, has over the years acquired something of an unexpected reputation as a wit, thanks to the oft-repeated story that on his deathbed Queen Mary told him that when he was feeling better they could return to Bognor Regis where he had once recovered from a nasty bout of flu, to which the king was heard to mutter 'Bugger Bognor'.

Or so we are led to believe – though why he should at that moment have decided to take against a perfectly nice Sussex town where the bracing sea air did wonders for his poor health is hard to explain.

There is a story that the town elders approached the King's private secretary, Lord Stamfordham, asking if His Majesty would be prepared to honour the town by bestowing the suffix Regis on the name. The subject was duly raised and it was at that moment that the King uttered his immortal words. Lord Stamfordham duly informed the petitioners that 'His Majesty has been graciously pleased to grant your request.'

One feels he would have been much happier if his parting comment to his people had been, as some say it was, 'How is the Empire?' On the other hand, this might not have been the solution many would have preferred, since he could have been referring to the cinema of the same name in Leicester Square which, rumour has it, he and Queen Mary once visited incognito to see *Lady, Be Good* starring Fred Astaire.

Luckily his reputation as one of the nation's super-grumps remains intact, thanks to a nurse who, as she was administering a sedative, distinctly heard him growl, 'God damn you.'

Humphrey Bogart's last words, to his wife, Lauren Bacall, as she left to a bit of shopping, were 'Goodbye, kid. Hurry back,' though I'd still rather like to think they were 'I should never have switched from scotch to martinis.'

I have no idea who Louise-Marie-Thérèse de Saint Maurice, Comtesse de Vercellis was, nor have I bothered to find out, but good on her for breaking wind on her deathbed and saying, 'Good. A woman who can fart is not dead.'

Sadly, my favourite last words are, again, apocryphal, and I do not wish to bore you with the real version. Union General John Sedgwick, under fire from Confederate snipers at the Battle of Spotsylvania in 1864, may not have ended his distinguished life with the words, 'They couldn't hit an elephant at this dist—' but where would he be today if some bright spark hadn't decided that he did?

What succeeding generations may or may think about you when you're drifting off under the influence of some form of palliative sedation may not be at the top of everyone's lists of concerns, and I imagine many would be astonished at the outpourings of praise and affection that appear a few days later in the better newspapers. Not that that's much consolation to the recipients, unless they now know something we don't. And I'm beginning to think that's what's beginning to bother me more than anything.

Will I be compos mentis enough to depart with a witty and memorable quip on my lips à la Oscar Wilde and the wallpaper, or will it be something altogether more helpful, like the 1st Lord Grimthorpe's 'We're low on marmalade'?

One lives in hope.

We Have a Camper Van

I knew a couple who, when they reached their seventies, were so bored with thinking of what to eat for supper that they decided to make do with something that was tasty, reasonably nourishing, and required minimal preparation.

The result was that every evening they sat down in front of the telly with a tray each, comprising two slices of lightly browned wholemeal and Primula cheese spread, which comes in a squeezable tube, and was always referred to by them as toothpaste on toast.

While it is widely accepted that we all lose our appetites as we get older, it is reassuring to learn that many of the tastes that we enjoyed in our childhood are not only still available, but as much enjoyed as ever.

According to a new survey (a phrase that covers more or less any fact or statistic that anyone chooses to air these days), marmalade is becoming the preserve of the old. Sixty per cent of marmalade sales in Britain go to people aged over sixty-five, while only one per cent of under-twenty-eights buy, or presumably eat, one of the great cornerstones of the English breakfast.

There is no obvious explanation for this gastronomic bombshell. One must assume that a lot of it is down to the fact that young people don't eat breakfast any more – at least not in the sense that we all did in our day as a matter of course.

The full English is, rightly, confined to weekends and holidays in hotels – mainly abroad. Or possibly to stately homes, though my evidence for this is largely anecdotal. But, as everyone knows, breakfast is the most important meal of the day. We miss it at our peril.

Speaking personally, a morning that does not begin with a bowl of cereal, toast and marmalade, and a pot of coffee is a morning wasted. But then, like many oldies, I realise I am becoming increasingly stuck in my ways, gastronomically speaking.

In 1959 a friend and I went to see a show called *Pieces of Eight* at the Apollo Theatre in London. This intimate revue was written by Peter Cook, with contributions from Harold Pinter and Sandy Wilson, and starred Kenneth Williams and Fenella Fielding.

The late fifties saw the arrival in Britain of continental restaurants, and one sketch, starring Williams, featured a terrible xenophobe who takes his date to one called the Bon Gourmet, where he tells the head waiter to 'stop speaking with that ridiculous regional accent' and turns down every dish he's offered.

Having dismissed hors d'oeuvres as 'leftovers in garlic', he then has a go at the minestrone. 'That Italian slop. A lot of gigolos and wops all mincing about with olive oil on their hair. We can see the sort of soup they'd make, can't we? Haven't you got a decent Brown Windsor, the soup of kings?'

Of course we both fell about laughing and went off afterwards for a sweet and sour in the nearest Chinese.

Even when I became the restaurant critic for *Vogue* magazine in the eighties, just as nouvelle cuisine arrived, I never really enjoyed my ventures into the gastronomic unknown (purely for the benefit of my readers) and now find myself becoming more Kenneth Williams-like by the day.

This is not so much out of fear for the effect that foreign spices and unusual sauces might have on my increasingly nervous stomach as because I like plain food, and always have.

I am far from alone. Occasionally invited to carve the Sunday joint by my late father-in-law, he never failed to remind me when it came to his turn to be served, 'Well done, outside, lean.'

He came from a long and proud tradition of Englishmen who knew what they liked when it came to food and liked what they knew, and, had he still been alive, he would have been the first to draw the family's attention to the story of Mr and Mrs Loftus – Phyllis, ninety-four, and George, one hundred, who earlier this year celebrated their seventy-seventh wedding anniversary. They currently enjoy the distinction of being the longest-married couple in England, and when asked for the secret of a good marriage Phyllis replied that in her experience the way to a man's heart is through his stomach.

'Always keep your husband well fed,' she advised. 'As long as there's good food on the table, that's all that matters.'

George, we are told, loves nothing better than a good roast dinner on Sunday, and for the rest of the week they have fish and shepherd's pie, as they have done every night of their marriage.

They have also carefully avoided smoking and drinking and owning a car and, as Phyllis's mother advised them seventy-five years ago, if you can afford something you like the look of when you're out shopping, go for it, but if not, 'shut your purse'.

Much has been written on the subject of love: how to find it, how to keep it, how not to go looking for it elsewhere, how to sustain it through the travails and tribulations of old age.

All manner of subjects and situations have been explored by all manner of writers – though too rarely do they touch on one area of marital love which many of us older couples are lucky enough to enjoy. I speak of companionship.

'The first time you marry for love,' said Jackie Kennedy. 'The second for money. And the third for companionship.'

Cynics might suggest that a woman who married only twice might not have been ideally placed to make such a sweeping observation. On the other hand, not every woman can claim to have achieved two out of their three objectives and she might be thought to be in a better position than most to suggest the third. At all events, I doubt many who have managed to stick together through thick and thin and are currently making old bones together would disagree with the view that once sex has lost its iron grip, there's no joy like companionship.

Sadly, not everyone stays the course long enough to experience that joy, but those that do are, more often than not, couples who have had a long and happy marriage already.

Ask them how they achieved a lifetime of bliss and the answers are charmingly simple. 'Kissing and hugging'; 'Sitting and chatting'; 'Not arguing about trivial things'; 'Having fun together'; 'Having a similar sense of humour'; 'Sitting down with a cup of tea and talking to each other ... '

P. G. Wodehouse once wrote that 'There is no surer foundation for a beautiful friendship than a mutual taste in literature.' To which one might add music, golf, gardening, travel, painting, charity work, jogging, walking in the countryside, dogs, sailing, baking cakes, watching television ... need I go on?

I know at least one elderly couple whose greatest pleasure is to sit of an evening listening to classical music while weaving tapestries.

Only one couple out of the many I questioned on the subject in a brief survey came up with a solution that would not have occurred to many.

'We have a camper van,' the wife said. 'We've had it for years and we go everywhere in it. If you can't get on in a camper van, you're not going to get on at all.'

'A camper van?' said Ludo. 'Bor-ring. I don't think *I* could get on with anyone in a camper van.'

'You haven't been married to someone for fifty years. If you had, you might find it really nice and cosy. And quite exciting when you think about it. The world's your oyster with a camper van.'

'I once tasted an oyster,' he said. 'It was disgusting.'

'Oysters are an acquired taste,' I said. 'Like caviar. And old champagne.'

'And camper vans.'

'And camper vans.'

'I can't imagine being old.'

'Neither can I,' I said.

'Even though you've written a book about it?'

'It doesn't mean I'm an expert on the subject. I'll know when I'm old, and so will you. Until then . . .'

'What?'

'Bash on, as Granny's father used to say.'

'Bash on, Grandpa.'